THE ROOSEVELT DIPLOMACY
AND WORLD WAR II

THE COMING OF THE WAR
IN THE PACIFIC, 1939-1941

1000 MILES

ARCTIC OCEAN

ALASKA (U.S.A.)

SOVIET UNION

S I B E R I A

Yakutsk

KAMCHATKA

SEA OF OKHOTSK

LAKE BAIKAL

Novo-Sibirsk

Irkutsk

Chita

SAKHALIN

KARAFUTO

KURILE IS. (JAP.)

ETOROFU

Ulan Bator

MONGOLIA

INNER MONGOLIA

MANCHUKUO

Khabarovsk

Vladivostok

6 — DEPARTURE OF PEARL HARBOR STRIKING FORCE NOV. 26, 1941

Harbin

SINKIANG

Mukden

Peking

Tientsin

Dairen

SEA OF JAPAN

KOREA

NORTH

TIBET

Lhasa

CHINA

Chungking

HUANG HO

YANGTSE

Nanking

Shanghai

PACIFIC

JAPANESE EMPIRE

Tokyo

BURMA ROAD

Foochow

EAST CHINA SEA

1 — BOMBING OF PANAY DEC. 12, 1937

BONIN IS. (JAP.)

OCEAN

INDIA (BR.)

Amoy

Canton

RYUKYU ISLANDS

13 — HONG KONG FALLS DEC. 25, 1941

FORMOSA

SOUTH

BURMA (BR.)

Rangoon

Hanoi

HAINAN

2 — OCCUPIED BY JAPS FEB. 10, 1939

8 — JAP LANDINGS DEC. 10, 1941

MARIANAS (JAP.)

PACIFIC

THAILAND

Bangkok

FRENCH INDOCHINA

4 — JAPS OCCUPY N. INDOCHINA SEPT. 22, 1940

LUZON

PHILIPPINE IS. (U.S.A.)

GUAM (U.S.A.)

9 — JAP LANDINGS DEC. 10, 1941

KRA ISTHMUS

Saigon

CAMRANH BAY

5 — JAPS OCCUPY S. INDOCHINA JULY 24, 1941

3 — JAPS OCCUPY SPRATLY I. MAR. 13, 1939

MINDANAO

YAP

(JAPANESE MANDATE)

PALAU

CAROLINE IS.

OCEAN

7 — JAP LANDINGS DEC. 8, 1941

12 — JAP LANDINGS DEC. 24, 1941

BR. N. BORNEO

11 — JAP LANDINGS DEC. 20, 1941

MALAY STATES (BR.)

10 — JAP LANDINGS DEC. 16, 1941

SARAWAK (BR.)

14 — SINGAPORE FALLS FEB. 15, 1942

BORNEO

CELEBES

SUMATRA

(AUSTR. MANDATE)

D U T C H   E A S T   I N D I E S

NEW GUINEA

PAPUA (AUSTR.)

INDIAN OCEAN

Batavia

JAVA

TIMOR (PORT.)

Darwin

AUSTRALIA

TRN

THE ROOSEVELT DIPLOMACY AND WORLD WAR II

Edited by ROBERT DALLEK
University of California, Los Angeles

HOLT, RINEHART AND WINSTON
New York · Chicago · San Francisco · Atlanta
Dallas · Montreal · Toronto · London · Sydney

Cover illustration: President Roosevelt with General Giraud, Winston Churchill and General de Gaulle at Casablanca, January 1943. *(Pix Incorporated)*

Maps on pp. ii and vi: From *The Growth of American Foreign Policy,* by Richard W. Leopold, two maps by Theodore R. Miller. © Copyright 1962 by Richard W. Leopold. Reproduced by permission of Alfred A. Knopf, Inc.

Copyright © 1970 by Holt, Rinehart and Winston, Inc.
All Rights Reserved
Library of Congress Catalog Card Number: 79–102986
SBN: 03–077260–5
Printed in the United States of America
9 8 7 6 5 4 3 2 1

CONTENTS

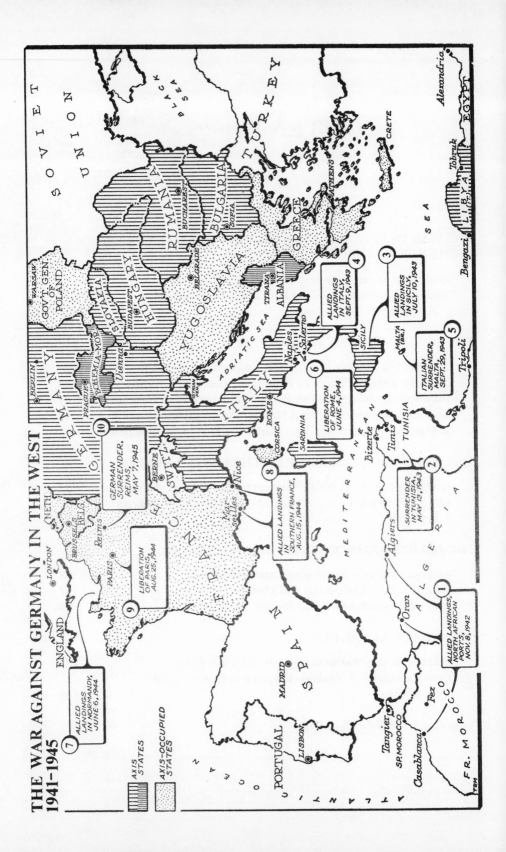

THE WAR AGAINST GERMANY IN THE WEST 1941-1945

AXIS STATES

AXIS-OCCUPIED STATES

SOVIET UNION

TURKEY

EGYPT

L I B Y A

Alexandria

Tobruk

Bengazi

Tripoli

GERMANY

GOV'T GEN. OF POLAND

WARSAW

BERLIN

PRAGUE

BOHEMIA-MORAVIA

SLOVAKIA

Vienna

BUDAPEST

HUNGARY

RUMANIA

BUCHAREST

BULGARIA

SOFIA

YUGOSLAVIA

BELGRADE

GREECE

ATHENS

CRETE

ALBANIA

TIRANA

ADRIATIC SEA

BLACK SEA

ITALY

ROME

Naples

Salerno

SARDINIA

CORSICA

SICILY

Nice

Marseilles

SWITZ.

BERNE

Reims

PARIS

FRANCE

SPAIN

MADRID

LISBON

PORTUGAL

ENGLAND

LONDON

BRUSSELS

BELG.

NETH.

HOL.

BrennerPass

MEDITERRANEAN SEA

MALTA (BR.)

TUNISIA

Bizerte

Tunis

ALGERIA

Algiers

Oran

MOROCCO

SP. MOROCCO

Tangier

Fez

Casablanca

FR. MOROCCO

ATLANTIC OCEAN

1 ALLIED LANDINGS, NORTH AFRICAN PORTS, NOV. 8, 1942

2 SURRENDER IN TUNISIA, MAY 13, 1943

3 ALLIED LANDINGS IN SICILY, JULY 10, 1943

4 ALLIED LANDINGS IN ITALY, SEPT. 9, 1943

5 ITALIAN SURRENDER, MALTA, SEPT. 29, 1943

6 LIBERATION OF ROME, JUNE 4, 1944

7 ALLIED LANDINGS IN NORMANDY, JUNE 6, 1944

8 ALLIED LANDINGS IN SOUTHERN FRANCE, AUG. 15, 1944

9 LIBERATION OF PARIS, AUG. 25, 1944

10 GERMAN SURRENDER, REIMS, MAY 7, 1945

TRM

INTRODUCTION

Few episodes in American history have generated as much controversy as World War II. The causes of American involvement, the Pearl Harbor disaster, the wartime leadership of the United States, the consequences of unconditional surrender, and American diplomacy at Yalta are subjects of enduring debate.

In a sense the argument over United States foreign policy and World War II began immediately after World War I. Disillusioned with the outcome of the peace negotiations and foreseeing new European troubles, a majority of Americans desired a return to traditional isolation from European power politics. But with some citizens still arguing for Wilsonian collective security, policymakers in the 1920s struck a compromise: the country rejected the League of Nations and specific military or political commitments, while at the same time energetically promoting reduced armaments and paper promises against war through measures like the Washington Conference of 1921–1922 and the Kellogg-Briand Pact of 1928.

When fascist aggression in the 1930s revealed the hollowness of moral commitments to peace, Americans embarked upon an all-out effort to isolate themselves from another war. Spurred on by the conviction that the country had been needlessly drawn into World War I, they demanded and received legislative guarantees against the conditions and policies that had apparently involved them in the earlier fighting. Taking the form of neutrality laws passed between 1935 and 1937, these restrictions included a mandatory embargo on the export of arms and munitions to a belligerent power, prohibited the transportation of such materials in American vessels, denied private citizens the right to grant loans and credits to belligerent states, and forbade Americans to travel on belligerent ships. Though some voices in the United States called for official action in the 1930s on behalf of China, Ethiopia, and Spain, and though President Franklin Roosevelt asked for power to discriminate between aggressors and victims of aggression in applying the arms embargo, most Americans were content with the neutrality laws, seeing them as a wall between themselves and warring states.

The outbreak of World War II went far to undermine this attitude. Openly sympathetic to Britain and France and fearful that a German victory might threaten their security, Americans generally lined up behind the idea of limited aid to the Allies. Consequently, in November 1939 the Congress legalized previously prohibited exports to belligerents on the condition that the exports be paid for in cash and carried away in foreign ships. Since Britain and France controlled the Atlantic sea lanes, the Allies were expected to be the only beneficiaries of this change in law, and until the spring of 1940, with the struggle more or less dead-locked, Americans saw little need to extend further aid. But Germany's conquest at that time of western Europe, including France, worked a dramatic change in attitude, convincing a majority of Americans that Germany rather than the Allies would probably win the war and that the United States must now extend all-out aid to Britain. Moreover, the disturbing Nazi successes moved President Roosevelt to pledge "to the opponents of force the material resources of this nation," signi-fying a commitment to transform American policy from neutrality to nonbelliger-ency, or indirect participation in the war.

Although the President's pledge was followed by shipments to Britain of vast quantities of World War I equipment, this was done through private firms and American neutrality under international law was technically maintained. The first clear-cut shift to nonbelligerency came with the destroyer–naval base deal of Sep-tember 1940. Exchanging fifty overage destroyers for bases in British possessions in the Western Hemisphere, Roosevelt openly placed the United States on the side of Britain in the fighting. Though the President appreciated that such behavior threat-ened the United States with full involvement in the conflict, he, like the public in general, believed that providing Britain with all aid short of war would give the country its best chance of staying out of the fighting. In line with this and the fact that Britain was running out of funds with which to pay "cash" for American weapons, Roosevelt and the Congress created the Lend-Lease Act of March 1941, by which the President was empowered to sell, lend, or lease defense articles to countries whose existence he deemed vital to the United States.

The issue now became how to assure the safe shipment of Lend-Lease goods. With German submarines sinking great numbers of merchant vessels, Roosevelt assigned the navy to warn British and neutral convoys of the presence of German warcraft in the area between the United States and the mid-Atlantic. Following this in July with the military occupation of Iceland and the introduction of naval escorts for American and Icelandic freighters traveling between the two countries, the President took the occasion of the Atlantic Conference in August to promise Winston Churchill an extension of the same protection to British merchant vessels. When an American warship exchanged fire with a German submarine at the beginning of September, the President used the incident both to fulfill his promise to Churchill and to introduce a shoot-on-sight policy against German and Italian war vessels in American defensive waters. The final step in this undeclared war between the Axis and the United States in the Atlantic occurred in November with repeal of the provisions of the neutrality law prohibiting the arming of American cargo ships, their travel into combat zones, and their delivery of goods to bellig-erent ports. At the same time, and as an extension of the effort to prevent a German victory in the war, Roosevelt declared Russia, which had been attacked by Hitler in June, vital to the defense of the United States and therefore eligible for Lend-Lease aid.

Throughout this period, while the Roosevelt Administration moved from a policy of limited assistance to all-out aid to the Allies short of war, the American public never ceased debating the merits of the Administration's diplomacy. Interventionists, who believed it more important for the United States to aid Britain than to stay out of war, supported the President with the argument that Britain was the country's first line of defense and that support of Britain was likely to stave off rather than bring involvement in the fighting. Isolationists or noninterventionists, who thought it more essential for the United States to avoid war than to save Britain or assure an Axis defeat, opposed Administration policy as leading the country directly into war. To combat this argument and to reassure the public, the President repeatedly promised to keep the United States out of the war as long as the country was not attacked.

While interventionists and isolationists debated the best foreign policy to pursue, they also argued about which group had the greatest public backing. Because opinion polls showed that a majority of the public consistently expressed a willingness to aid Britain even at the risk of war, the interventionists contended that the Administration's policies represented the majority will. Because opinion polls also showed that 80 percent of Americans opposed a declaration of war and full belligerency, the noninterventionists described their policy of neutrality as a more honest expression of the public mood. Moreover, because the President continually pledged to keep the country out of war when it was clear that his policies might well bring involvement, isolationists contended that Roosevelt consciously misled the public. Who, then, was right? Was the public for aid short of war or for neutrality? Did Roosevelt willfully deceive Americans into thinking they could steer clear of war when he believed otherwise? And if he was not entirely candid with the public about foreign affairs, can this be construed as an effort to lead the country into the war? The first two readings debate these points.

Charles A. Beard, a famous American historian and leading noninterventionist before Pearl Harbor, continued to argue after 1945 that the American people had above all wanted peace and that their response to President Roosevelt's promise, especially during the 1940 election campaign, to keep the country out of foreign wars testifies strongly to this fact. Beard also states that Roosevelt, though appreciating this, decided shortly before or after the outbreak of war that it would be necessary to involve the United States in the conflict and that despite his pledges to the contrary he systematically worked toward this end. How does Beard attempt to show that the President deceitfully tried to bring the country into the war? Does the fact that the United States entered the conflict only after it was attacked—a condition Roosevelt repeatedly singled out as the only ground on which the nation would fight—raise any questions about Beard's thesis?

William L. Langer and S. Everett Gleason express a view at issue with that of

Beard. These historians contend that American support for a policy of aid to the Allies was widespread and that by September 1940, the time of the destroyer–naval base deal, the majority of Americans were ready to proceed to any lengths to defeat the Axis. Moreover, they assert that although the President did not always deal candidly with the public in matters relating to the war and although he occasionally expressed anxiety about the nation's ability to avoid involvement in the fighting, he consistently aimed and worked to prevent such involvement. How do Langer and Gleason explain the discrepancy between an "any lengths" attitude in September 1940 and the continuing majority opposition to full belligerency? How do they counter the argument that Roosevelt's failure to be entirely candid with the public is evidence that he worked to bring the country into the war? Do they prove that Roosevelt respected public opinion?

These questions cannot be answered without taking into account developments in the Far East, where the full-scale involvement of the United States actually began.

The touchstone of the national policy in the Far East, dating to the turn of the century, was the open door for China, or a policy of opposition to any impairment of Chinese territorial or political integrity and to any foreign economic or political monopoly of influence. This principle was reaffirmed in the Nine-Power Treaty of 1922 and in the Hoover-Stimson doctrine of 1932 which refused recognition of Japan's territorial gains in Manchuria. The advent of the Roosevelt Administration brought no change in approach: Japan's resumption of military aggression against China in July 1937, with subsequent destruction of American lives and property, moved the President to speak publicly of quarantining aggressors, to extend material aid to China, and to issue a declaration of intent in July 1939 to terminate the existing Japanese-American commercial treaty as a means of controlling the flow of war supplies to Tokyo. Though the treaty was allowed to lapse in January 1940, the Administration did not reduce the export of strategic materials until the summer and fall, when Japan began exploiting Hitler's victories over the Allies in Europe with successful demands upon the British, Dutch, and French for concessions in the Far East. Tokyo's reply was the Tripartite Pact of September 27, which essentially warned the United States that involvement in fighting with either Germany or Japan would mean a war with all three of the Axis states. Instead of intimidating the Roosevelt Administration into reducing its aid to Britain and China, the Pact intensified American feeling against the fascist states and encouraged the development of the Lend-Lease program at the beginning of 1941. Moreover, it did nothing to discourage American planning for combined action with Britain and Holland in case of war, or to prevent the Administration from answering the Japanese acquisition of French bases in southern Indochina in July with an embargo on almost all war supplies, including, most importantly, oil.

With relations almost at a breaking point in the summer of 1941, the two sides began an exchange of suggestions for negotiating their differences over Japan's thrust to the south, the future of China, and trade in strategic materials: in September, Japanese Premier Prince Konoye proposed a summit conference, which Roosevelt and Secretary of State Cordell Hull rejected when Konoye refused commitments to a preliminary understanding; in November, the new and more militant Tojo Cabinet made two proposals, known as A and B, which Roosevelt and Hull also rejected and replied to on November 26 with suggestions of their own unacceptable to Japan. This diplomatic impasse set in motion a Japanese war plan which ended with the successful surprise attack on Pearl Harbor on December 7 and German-Italian declarations of war against the United States four days later.

This series of events is the subject of the second group of readings which present differing interpretations of the role of American policy in producing the conflict with Japan. Herbert Feis, a member of the Roosevelt Administration and the most prolific American writer on World War II diplomacy, argues that the origins of the war with Japan can be found chiefly in Tokyo's attempt to establish its hegemony in East Asia. Although Feis acknowledges shortcomings in American diplomacy in the Far East in 1939–1941, he strongly contends that Administration policies such as economic sanctions and the rejection of Japanese negotiating proposals in 1941 were restrained and realistic replies to Japanese aggression.

Anthony Kubek, a political scientist and an articulate exponent of the revisionist critique of Roosevelt diplomacy during World War II, sharply challenges Feis's picture of events. In Kubek's view, American policy in the Far East was designed to provoke war. The chief motives Kubek sees for this design were a desire on the part of pro-Soviet Administration officials to save Russia from a Japanese attack and a conviction on the part of Roosevelt and Hull that war with Japan would bring American involvement in the European fighting, which they believed necessary to assure a German defeat.

Paul Schroeder takes a middle ground between Feis and Kubek. While failing to see any sinister design or warlike intent in Administration policy toward Japan, he does see an inflexibility of approach which destroyed the chance for a negotiated settlement in the latter half of 1941 and unintentionally provoked the Japanese into a military assault. What does Schroeder describe as inflexible in American policy? And how does his explanation of the origins of the war compare with those of Feis and Kubek?

The question of responsibility for the conflict is closely tied to the debate on surprise and defeat at Pearl Harbor. For defenders of the Administration who could find no blame in American diplomacy for the collapse of Japanese-American negotiations, the attack on Pearl Harbor was a confirmation of Japanese wickedness or the logical climax to a decade of unprovoked Japanese aggression against peaceful peoples and states. But because such an attack was supposedly in character with previous Japanese behavior, many Americans expressed bewilderment at the military's unpreparedness and defeat. The charges of a presidential board of inquiry in 1942 and of a joint congressional committee in 1945–1946 that local army and navy field commanders performed inadequately, committing errors of judgment, supported this view. Because these investigations could be seen as contrived exonerations of Washington officials and because they brought evidence to light of forewarnings to high officials of a Pearl Harbor assault, some Administration critics found support for the suspicion that the Pearl Harbor disaster was part of a plot to involve the United States in the war. Or, as stated in revisionist literature on Roosevelt diplomacy, though the Administration foresaw the attack, it purposely failed to alert Pearl Harbor defenders, thus assuring a military disaster that would unify the nation behind a commitment to join the Allies in the fighting. This is the thrust of George Morgenstern's essay on the causes of the Pearl Harbor defeat.

An answer to Morgenstern and others blaming local field chiefs comes from Roberta Wohlstetter. After studying American intelligence operations in 1941, she concluded that Pearl Harbor was the fault of no single individual or group of individuals but rather the result of a national failure to anticipate. Wohlstetter argues that despite an abundance of "signals" pointing to a Pearl Harbor attack, the American government was unable to perceive them as such. Moreover, she contends that even if the "signals" had been heard, satisfactory preparations to cope with the assault would not necessarily have been forthcoming. Why and how this was so forms the substance of her discussion.

The diplomacy of the United States after its entry into World War II is a subject of historical controversy as intense as that which centers about events leading to its involvement. In its most general form the debate has focused on the cause of postwar communist domination of western Europe and East Asia— whether due to wartime blunders or to circumstances beyond American control.

A central issue in the discussion has been the nature of the wartime leadership of the United States. Chester Wilmot, an Australian journalist with a broad knowledge of European military and diplomatic history during World War II, argues that the chief goal of American diplomacy was to substitute an international peacekeeping body for traditional prewar empires, alliances, and spheres of influence. In Wilmot's view, such a strategy was based on naïve and unrealistic assumptions. Arthur Schlesinger, Jr. also sees the Roosevelt Administration as aiming to lead the international community away from balance-of-power and sphere-of-interest diplomacy, but he contends that this "universalist" approach to postwar peacekeeping had much to recommend it on both idealistic and realistic grounds. How do Wilmot and Schlesinger support their respective conclusions?

A more specific point of debate in the argument over wartime diplomacy concerns the United States policy of unconditional surrender. The background to this issue involves the history of the country's wartime relations with the Soviet Union and, more specifically, President Roosevelt's conception of what was needed to maintain a solid alliance against the Axis states.

From the outset of the war the Roosevelt Administration committed itself to a Europe-first strategy, that is, a determination to defeat Germany and Italy before Japan. Though honoring this commitment in 1942 by marshaling American strength primarily against Germany, including the invasion of North Africa, the combined Anglo-American effort did not include a promised direct assault on France which would have relieved Russian troops, who bore the brunt of the fighting in the east. Because of a long history of strained relations between the U.S.S.R. and its Western allies, Stalin took this as a sign of bad faith, and this strengthened his suspicions of a Western policy of German defeat at Russian expense. Moreover, the failure of the Allies to open a second front in Europe in 1942 along with American dealings with Vichy France, Hitler's collaborator, aroused Stalin's fear that the United States and Britain would make a separate peace with Germany to assure limitations on Russian power. Eager to reassure Stalin that none of this was the case and hoping to inhibit inclinations of the Russians to make their own separate arrangements with Germany, Roosevelt and Churchill took the occasion of the Casablanca Conference in January 1943 to announce a policy of unconditional surrender, or determination to fight the war through to Germany's complete defeat. Roosevelt hoped, furthermore, that such a policy would save the Allies from Wilson's error of seeking surrender through specific unrealizable post-war promises which, as after World War I, could then become a rallying point for nationalism and renewed aggression.

This policy of unconditional surrender has been attacked on a number of grounds. Anne Armstrong suggests that it was a moralistic, inflexible idea based more on wartime passions than considered postwar political aims. John L. Snell and Paul Kecskemeti take a fundamentally different view. Snell sees the unconditional surrender formula as the outgrowth of high-level discussions and as a useful policy. Kecskemeti depicts its impact on Germany as considerably less substantial than Armstrong believes. How do these writers arrive at such different conclusions?

The unconditional surrender policy, then, was partly an attempt to solve the Allied problem of assuring cooperation with Russia for German defeat. Another wartime problem for Britain and the United States in their dealings with Russia was how to promote postwar cooperation without excessively jeopardizing their interests. The major points at issue were four: the treatment of Germany; the fate of Eastern Europe, particularly Poland for whose defense England and France had first entered the war; the establishment of an international peacekeeping body; and the redistribution of power in East Asia after Japan's defeat. Though Churchill, Roosevelt, and Stalin exchanged opinions on these questions in the months after all had entered the war, their first face-to-face discussion of these political problems came at Teheran in November and December 1943. But with the military victory still unassured and discussions of such items as German and Polish destinies raising troublesome tensions, the heads of state deferred specific decisions to a future time.

That time and place was February 1945 at Yalta in the Russian Crimea. There, the Big Three agreed to disarm, demilitarize, and dismember Germany "as they deem requisite for future peace and security"; ratified an earlier commitment to joint occupation of Berlin, though no rights of access were established; and agreed to make Germany pay reparations, taking a $20 billion sum as a basis for later discussion. On Poland, the powers agreed to establish new boundaries and arrange for the organization of a provisional government and subsequent "free and unfettered elections." The future of other Eastern European states was dealt with through a Declaration on Liberated Europe in which peoples liberated from Nazi rule were promised help in forming freely chosen democratic governments. The creation of a United Nations organization, to which the Roosevelt Administration gave the highest priority, was advanced to the charter-writing stage with the resolution of major differences remaining from the Dumbarton Oaks Conference of 1944. And lastly, questions about postwar conditions in East Asia were settled in a secret protocol in which Russia was granted a variety of concessions in return for which Stalin agreed to enter the war against Japan after Germany surrendered and to conclude a pact of friendship and alliance with the Nationalist Government of China.

No aspect of wartime diplomacy has created more controversy than Yalta. Failing to assure the postwar cooperation of the United States and the Soviet Union, to make nations free and secure, or, as Roosevelt promised, to do away with spheres of influence, alliances, and balance-of-power diplomacy, the Yalta agreements have been vulnerable to the sharpest kind of attack. William Henry Chamberlin offers a good example of how Yalta critics have taken the President and the agreements to task. Likewise, Sidney Warren provides a concise statement of the argument used in defense, explaining not that Yalta was a triumph of American diplomacy but why the Administration could not have done better.

Neither one of the selections on Yalta nor any other reading in this book is likely to satisfy the reader's desire for a clear-cut, convincing explanation of events. But, the thoughtful student will ask, could a book on American wartime diplomacy end on any other note? The answer would seem to be no, for as with other great historical episodes, the story of Roosevelt diplomacy and World War II is replete with contradictions which will undoubtedly continue to give rise to discussion and debate.

In the reprinted selections footnotes appearing in the original sources have in general been omitted unless they contribute to the argument or better understanding of the selection.

Long before he became involved in the debate over Franklin Roosevelt's diplomacy, CHARLES A. BEARD (1874–1948) had established himself as one of America's great historians. His *An Economic Interpretation of the Constitution* (1913) and *The Rise of American Civilization* (2 vols., 1927) secured his reputation among both professionals and laymen. In the 1930s he was a leading spokesman for an isolationist foreign policy, and in the 1940s he became the leading revisionist writer on American pre-war diplomacy with publication of *American Foreign Policy in the Making, 1932–1940* (1946) and *President Roosevelt and the Coming of the War, 1941* (1948). In this last work, from which the following selection is drawn, Beard raises serious questions about Roosevelt's honesty in explaining his foreign policy to the American people.*

Charles A. Beard

Roosevelt Deceived the Public

President Roosevelt entered the year 1941 carrying moral responsibility for his covenants with the American people to keep this nation out of war—so to conduct foreign affairs as to avoid war. Those covenants, made in the election campaign of 1940, were of two kinds. The first were the pledges of the Democratic party to which he publicly subscribed while he was bidding for the suffrages of the people. The second were his personal promises to the people, supplementing the obligations of his party's platform.

The antiwar covenants of the Democratic party, to which President Roosevelt had committed himself unreservedly during the campaign, were clear-cut: "We will not participate in foreign wars, and we will not send our Army, naval, or air forces to fight in foreign lands outside of the Americas, except in case of attack. . . . The direction and aim of our foreign policy has been, and will continue to be, the security and defense of our own land and the maintenance of its peace."

In supplementing the pledges of the Democratic platform, President Roosevelt had also been unequivocal in his personal declarations. At Philadelphia, October 23, 1940, he had branded as false a Republican charge that "this Administration wishes to lead this country into war," and proclaimed that he was "following the road to peace." At Boston on October 30, he was even more emphatic, for there he declared: "I have said this before, but I

*From Charles A. Beard, *President Roosevelt and the Coming of the War, 1941,* pp. 3–9, 407, 409–415, 574–575, 582–584. Copyright, 1948, by Yale University Press. Footnotes omitted.

shall say it again and again and again: Your boys are not going to be sent into any foreign wars. . . . The purpose of our defense is defense." At Buffalo, November 2, his vow was short and unqualified: "Your President says this country is not going to war."

It is true that the Democratic platform of 1940 pledged to liberty-loving peoples wantonly attacked "all the material aid at our command, consistent with law and not inconsistent with the interests of our own national self-defense." It is true also that during the campaign President Roosevelt reiterated, reinforced, and enlarged upon this promise. But neither Democratic party leaders nor President Roosevelt at the time construed the pledge to extend, conditionally, material aid to liberty-loving peoples as canceling the conditions and their anti-war covenants. And indeed it would require more than casuistry to show that an indefinite and conditional pledge in fact obliterated *ex vi termini* definite and unequivocal pledges to the contrary made simultaneously and subsequently.

On their part, the Republicans and their candidate, Wendell Willkie, likewise committed themselves to definite promises that they would keep the United States out of war. The antiwar plank of the Republican platform read: "The Republican party is firmly opposed to involving this nation in foreign war." While expressing a real fear that the Administration was heading for war, Mr. Willkie reiterated again and again and again during the campaign a solemn promise that if elected President no American boys would be sent to fight in any European or Asiatic war.

Whatever secret reservations President Roosevelt and Mr. Willkie may have cherished when they made their antiwar commitments to the American people, there can be no doubt about the unequivocal nature of their covenants to keep the country out of war if victorious at the polls. Nor could there be any doubt that the overwhelming majority of the American people were then convinced that the United States should stay out of war in Europe and Asia. That conviction had long been maturing, in a large measure as the result of experiences during and after World War I. . . .

Had President Roosevelt been privately convinced in 1940 that the United States should enter the war, he knew, as well as Mr. Willkie did, that the sentiment of the Democratic party, and of the country, was almost solidly against that view. Only a small proportion of the delegates at the Republican convention at Philadelphia in June dared to reveal opinions veering in the direction of war for the United States and all such opinions were quickly overridden by the resolute majority of non-interventionists. At the Democratic convention in Chicago a few days later the antiwar sentiment among the delegates was even stronger, if possible, than it had been among the Republicans at Philadelphia; President Roosevelt and his agents bowed to that sentiment.

Indeed, in respect of foreign policy, the striking feature of the political campaign of 1940 was the predominance of the antiwar sentiment among Democrats and Republicans—the overwhelming majority of the American people. At no time during that contest did President Roosevelt or Mr. Willkie or any other responsible party leader venture to propose openly that the United States should become involved in foreign wars or should adopt measures calculated to result in war. On the contrary, as far as the two great parties were concerned, the only choice before the voters was between two candidates, President Roosevelt and Mr. Willkie, both engaged in outbidding each other in the solemnity and the precision of their pledges to maintain the neutrality and peace of the United States.

Nor must the circumstances in which their pledges were made be forgotten. Before the campaign of 1940 got into full swing France had fallen a victim to Hitler's conquering hordes, British armed forces had suffered disaster at Dunkirk, Germany seemed triumphant in western Europe, and Great Britain was beleaguered, daily expecting a German invasion. In other words, the peril of Britain seemed greater in the summer and autumn of 1940 than it did after June, 1941, when Hitler plunged into a war with Russia. Yet it was in those months of Britain's desperation in 1940 that President Roosevelt and Democratic candidates for Congress, pleading for the suffrages of the American people, promised that, if victorious, they would maintain the security and peace of the United States.

If the processes of popular election and responsible government had any meaning or validity, the antiwar covenants with the American people, freely entered into by the Democratic party and President Roosevelt during the campaign of 1940, were specific commitments to be fulfilled after their victory at the polls in November. Those covenants were explicit mandates for the President in the conduct of foreign affairs in 1941. They were equally explicit mandates for the Democratic Senators and Representatives, who had indubitable control of Congress, in the enactment of legislation relative to all issues of peace and war.

Those covenants were no mere incidents or practical jokes of the campaign. They were, in fact, major promises of the campaign, extensively and definitely expounded in documents and speeches, and were binding in honor and good conscience after the election. In short, unless deceiving the people in matters of life and death

is to be regarded as a proper feature of the democratic politics and popular decisions at the polls are to be treated as chimeras, President Roosevelt's peace pledges of 1940 were imperatives for him in 1941; and only by spurning the peace pledges of their party could Democratic Senators and Representatives dominant in Congress enact into law measures calculated to take the United States into war.

To this principle of representative government, admittedly, exceptions are allowable, for example, where a drastic and unexpected alteration in the posture of affairs calls for a change of policy after an election. If, however, President Roosevelt came to the conclusion in 1941 that his antiwar commitments of 1940 had been rendered obsolete by changed circumstances in 1941 and that the United States should engage in war, he was under constitutional and moral obligations to explain to the country the grounds and nature of a reversal in policy. It may be said, to be sure, and has been said by defenders of his course, that in many of his addresses in 1941 he declared that there was danger of war coming, danger of attacks upon the United States, and a growing need for more and more preparation for defense. Indeed he did assert publicly that Hitler had designs for conquering the world, suppressing all religions, destroying liberty, and subduing the American people. He did say, more than once, that Hitler intended to attack the United States and, after the "shooting war" had begun, that Hitler had attacked America. In some addresses also he claimed that, in the election returns of 1940 and the Lend-Lease Act, he had sanction for pursuing an almost unlimited policy in the conduct of foreign affairs; and such addresses could be and occasionally were interpreted by American advocates of war to be public announcements of his intention to push affairs to the extreme of war in support of the Allies if necessary to assure their victory over the Axis Powers.

But over against all his declarations about war dangers in 1941 and his claims to a sanction for pursuing an aggressive policy stood his other declarations in line with the antiwar pledges of 1940. Repeatedly, between January 1, 1941, and the middle of December, 1941, he represented his policy as a policy contrary to war, as a quest for the peace and security of the United States. Once during those months, that is, on November 29, 1941, it is true, he did say that within a year American boys might be fighting, but this utterance was vague and gave no indication that the fighting would be due to a change in his policy as proclaimed in 1940. . . .

At what point in time, if any, did President Roosevelt decide that the United States would, deliberately or of necessity, enter or become involved in the war and begin to make plans with this issue in view? Since he never called upon Congress for a declaration of war, until after the Japanese attack, or publicly announced such a decision on his part, this subject will long remain open to debate. . . .

As if fully sensitive to the fact that this question of time has a decisive bearing on President Roosevelt's antiwar pledges in 1940 and preceding years, as well as on the process by which the United States actually became involved in war, former officials of the Roosevelt Administration and other expositors of its measures have undertaken to meet the challenge. Referring to it in a review of my *American Foreign Policy in the Making, 1932–1940,* Adolf Berle, Jr., Assistant Secretary of State, 1938–44, and presumably possessing inside knowledge, said in 1946: "Somewhat rhetorically, on p. 45, it is asked, 'At what point in time of [during] these "fateful years" did the President and the Secretary (Hull)

decide that the policy of neutrality and isolationism . . . was untenable and announce to the public that another foreign policy—one opposed to it—was in the best interest of the United States?' "

Then Mr. Berle gave what he apparently regarded as an answer to the question: "The date when war was considered probable rather than remotely possible was shortly after the Munich conferences [1938]—up to which time the President and Secretary were hoping against hope that Europe at least would find a balance and solve its own problems. General disarmament after Munich was to be the acid test." When did the President announce to the country that the policy of neutrality and isolation had been abandoned for another policy? On this point Mr. Berle remarked:

This reviewer [Mr. Berle] would have thought that the records of the President and Mr. Hull were clear. Notable among the relevant documents are President Roosevelt's "quarantine speech" in 1937 [the year before Munich] and repeated warnings by Mr. Hull (many of which the author [Beard] omits) that Axis aggression, if continued, would endanger the safety of the United States as well as of the rest of the world. The growing and ever blunter expressions to foreign governments, instinct with American apprehension, plainly indicated the coming development. Historians may argue that clearer statements could have been made. Perhaps. But the country did not misunderstand.

Mr. Berle appeared to fix the date of the turn from neutrality and isolationism at some time in 1938 and cited President Roosevelt's quarantine speech of October 5, 1937, the previous year, as among the relevant documents. If October 5, 1937, is to be taken as the date of the turn, then it is to be noted that President Roosevelt at a press conference the following day, October 6, 1937, when asked whether the quarantine speech was "a repudiation" of the Neutrality Act, replied: "Not for a minute. It may be an expansion." If the date of the turn is to be fixed "shortly after" the Munich conferences in 1938, then what may be said of numerous reaffirmations of their adherence to peace and neutrality for the United States made publicly by President Roosevelt and Secretary Hull in 1939 and 1940?

Among the other "relevant documents" mentioned by Mr. Berle, in addition to the quarantine speech of October 5, 1937, were "repeated warnings" about Axis aggressions, and "the growing and ever blunter expressions to foreign governments" which "plainly indicated the coming development." But Mr. Berle cited no specific warning or expression that could be dated and analyzed with a view to discovering whether it "plainly indicated" a turn from or repudiation of the antiwar and proneutrality pledges of President Roosevelt and the Democratic party in 1939 and 1940. As if appreciating intellectual difficulties of explication, Mr. Berle stated that "historians may argue that plainer statements could have been made. Perhaps." Then he added: "But the country did not misunderstand."

As a matter of fact a careful examination of every sentence in all these addresses and speeches in the nature of warnings and ever blunter expressions yields no information on the point of time at which President Roosevelt had decided to abandon the policy of neutrality and announce that another foreign policy—one pointed in the direction of war—was in the best interest of the United States. Yet, for what it is worth and means, Mr. Berle's statement may be taken to imply that in 1937 or 1938 or thereabouts, President Roosevelt had decided that "war was considered probable," and hence that the maintenance of neutrality and peace for the

United States was improbable. Such at least seems to be the upshot of Mr. Berle's effort to enlighten "historians," if not "the country" on the point at issue. Even so, it is no answer to the question I posed.

In respect of this chronological problem, Sumner Welles, former Undersecretary of State, said in 1946:

> As I have earlier written, President Roosevelt since the autumn of 1936 had become ever more deeply engrossed with foreign policy. No matter how urgent the problems of domestic reform and recovery might be, he had long since recognized that neither recovery nor reform could be enduring in a world so rapidly rushing toward war. He was already obsessed with the dangers by which the United States was confronted. By the summer of 1941 *the dangers had become imminent. . . .* By the summer of 1941 the overwhelming issue was his need *to obtain the support of the people of the United States, and of their Congress,* for those measures which were indispensable if the United States *was to be prepared to defend herself should she be drawn into war* and if, in the meantime, she was to be able to render such assistance as was available to the British people then fighting alone against the Axis. Isolationist sentiment was still widespread. . . .

That President Roosevelt had made the fateful decision before the summer of 1940 was intimated by Mr. Justice Frankfurter in his memorial address at Harvard University in April, 1945:

> But there came a time when he [the President] could no longer doubt that he had to shift from the task of social reform to war leadership, in order not only to maintain our spiritual heritage but to assure opportunities for further progress as a free society.

There came a moment when President Roosevelt was convinced that the utter defeat of Nazism was essential to the survival of our institutions. That time certainly could not have been later than when Mr. Sumner Welles reported on his mission to Europe [March, 1940]. Certainly from the time that the fall of France seemed imminent, the President was resolved to do everything possible to prevent the defeat of the Allies. Although confronted with the obvious danger of attack by the Axis upon us, there came that series of bold and triumphant measures which Mr. Churchill authoritatively summarized in his recent moving speech to the House of Commons—the shipment of arms to Great Britain, the stab-in-the-back speech, the base-destroyer deal, lend-lease, the smoothing of the difficult ways of the Allied purchasing missions, the encouragement of Mr. Willkie's trip to England, the assistance in a hundred ways of British economic warfare, the extraordinarily prompt and cordial support of Russia. Moreover, while engaged in this series of complicated moves, he so skilfully conducted affairs as to avoid even the appearance of an act of aggression on our part.

And so, in the hour of national disaster on that Sunday afternoon after Japan had struck, when the President had gathered about him his cabinet and his military chiefs, the most experienced statesman among his advisers, after watching the President's powerful and self-possessed control of the situation, could say to himself, "There is my leader."

The question of the time when President Roosevelt accepted "the probability that the United States would have to enter the approaching European war" is treated by Alden Hatch in his *Franklin D. Roosevelt: An Informal Biography* (1947). Owing to the laudatory and imaginative nature of Mr. Hatch's work, any of his statements not otherwise supported by authentic documents, may, of course, be discounted by critics, but Mr. Hatch secured information from a number of distinguished persons, "intimates" of President Roosevelt in the prewar years; for example, Mrs. Roosevelt, Admiral William D. Leahy, Vice-Admiral Ross T. McIntire, Samuel I. Rosenman, Franklin D. Roosevelt, Jr., Josephus Daniels, Justice Felix Frankfurter, and Ernest K. Lindley.

Mr. Hatch states that Vice-Admiral McIntire was convinced that the President accepted "the probability that the United States would have to enter the approaching European war if the democratic way of life were to be saved," for the first time, just after he had received news of the Hitler-Stalin Pact in August, 1939. Mr. Hatch concedes that the President did not then say positively that such was his decision but Mr. Hatch declares this to be a reasonable assumption based on what the President actually said. This opinion, Mr. Hatch says, he checked with other advisers of the President—in addition to Vice-Admiral McIntire—and put to them the question: "When do you think that the President decided that the United States would probably have to enter the war?" In every instance, he reports, "the reply fixed the time within a few weeks of that day [August 23, 1939, the date of the Hitler-Stalin Pact]." . . .

The great end which President Roosevelt discerned and chose justified the means which he employed. As a farsighted statesman he early discovered that unless the United States entered the war raging in Europe, Hitler would be victorious; and the United States, facing alone this monstrous totalitarian power, would become a victim of its merciless ideology and its despotic militarism. According to this interpretation, it was a question of democracy, the Four Freedoms, the noble principles of the Atlantic Charter, and world security on the one side; of totalitarianism, consummate despotism, and military subjugation on the other side. Since the American people were so smug in their conceit, so ignorant of foreign affairs, and so isolationist in sentiment that they could not themselves see the reality of this terrible threat to their own safety and a necessity to meet it by a resort to war, President Roosevelt had to dissemble in order to be re-elected in 1940 as against Wendell

Willkie, then the antiwar candidate of the Republicans on an antiwar platform. Furthermore, as members of Congress, Democrats and Republicans alike, continued throughout the year, until December 7, their vigorous opposition to involvement in war, President Roosevelt, in conducting foreign affairs, had to maintain the appearance of a defensive policy until the Japanese attack on Pearl Harbor. But the means which President Roosevelt actually employed in the conduct of foreign affairs were justified by the great end which he, with peculiar clairvoyance had early discerned and chosen for himself and his country.

Oblique but evident support for this interpretation was provided by the Department of State in Chapter I of its publication, *Peace and War, 1931–1941,* issued in July, 1943, prepared by or for Secretary Hull. In that chapter, the President and the Secretary of State are represented as convinced at some time "early" in that decade that "the idea of isolation as expressed in 'neutrality' legislation" was untenable, as having information about foreign affairs or foreseeing developments in foreign relations of which the public was not aware, and as compelled to move gradually "to a position in the forefront of the United Nations that are making common cause against an attempt at world conquest unparalleled alike in boldness of conception and in brutality of operation." . . .

. . . If the precedents set by President Roosevelt in conducting foreign affairs . . . are to stand unimpeached and be accepted henceforth as valid in law and morals then:

The President of the United States in a campaign for reelection may publicly promise the people to keep the country out of war and, after victory at the polls, may set out secretly on a course designed or practically certain to bring war upon the country.

He may, to secure legislation in furtherance of his secret designs, misrepresent to Congress and the people both its purport and the policy he intends to pursue under its terms if and when such legislation is enacted. . . .

He may, after publicly announcing one foreign policy, secretly pursue the opposite and so conduct foreign and military affairs as to maneuver a designated foreign power into firing the first shot in an attack upon the United States and thus avoid the necessity of calling upon Congress in advance to exercise its constitutional power to deliberate upon a declaration of war. . . .

In short, if these precedents are to stand unimpeached and to provide sanctions for the continued conduct of American foreign affairs, the Constitution may be nullified by the President, officials, and officers who have taken the oath, and are under moral obligation, to uphold it. For limited government under supreme law they may substitute personal and arbitrary government—the first principle of the totalitarian system against which, it has been alleged, World War II was waged—while giving lip service to the principle of constitutional government.

No study of American diplomacy before Pearl Harbor is so extensive as that of WILLIAM L. LANGER (b. 1896), emeritus professor of history at Harvard University, and S. EVERETT GLEASON (b. 1905), a member of the Historical Division of the Department of State. Invited shortly after the war by the Council on Foreign Relations to undertake "an extensive, scholarly history of American foreign policy in the period just before and during the Second World War," Langer and Gleason published *The Challenge to Isolation, 1937–1940* (1952) and *The Undeclared War, 1940–1941* (1953), works which together constitute some seventeen hundred pages. The following selection is drawn from these books and takes issue with Beard on Roosevelt's response to public attitudes toward the war.*

William L. Langer and S. Everett Gleason

Roosevelt Respected Public Opinion

Like all successful Presidents, [Roosevelt] was of course an adroit and accomplished politician and never left Congress or the country out of his calculations. He realized that any foreign policy, if it were to succeed, must have the declared or at least tacit approval of Congress and the support of the public. Hostile writers have tried to prove him a would-be dictator and have emphasized his allegedly insidious maneuvers to steer the country into a policy bound to end in war. The record suggests, however, that while the President certainly gave intellectual leadership in arousing the country to the dangers of the world situation, he was often a temporizer when it came to action. Mrs. Roosevelt has

commented on her late husband's keen sense of timing and on his ability to await patiently the arrival of what seemed to him the most auspicious moment. She has remarked also on his feeling that no leader could afford to get too far ahead of his followers, and on his wholesome respect for the opinion of Congress as expressive of the popular sentiment.

These points seem to be well taken. Mr. Roosevelt certainly kept his political ear to the ground and at a rather early date decided for himself that systematic public-opinion polls were not sufficient for his purposes. He read a number of important newspapers every morning, including the most hostile. Knowledgeable citizens from

*In the following selection pages 16–21 are from William L. Langer and S. Everett Gleason, *The Challenge to Isolation, 1937–1940* (New York: Harper & Row, for the Council on Foreign Relations, 1952), pp. 5–6, 201–203, 770–772, 775–776. Pages 21–25 are from William L. Langer and S. Everett Gleason, *The Undeclared War, 1940–1941* (New York: Harper & Row, for the Council on Foreign Relations, 1953), pp. 198, 202, 205–207, 209, 211–212.

16

all parts of the country were received with pleasure and treated as important sources of information. Finally, he relied on his much-traveled wife to provide detailed reports on all sorts of conditions and trends throughout the land.

In retrospect, indeed, there is real ground for thinking that the President tended to underestimate popular support for his foreign policy and that his occasional reluctance to act or to act openly may have been occasioned by his misgivings about Congress, for which he evidently had an almost inordinate concern. It was, of course, true that in the years before Pearl Harbor there was in Congress much determined and bitter opposition to the Administration, on the score of both domestic and foreign policy. Nonetheless, on reviewing the record it is hard to escape the impression that the President was inclined to exaggerate the strength and cohesion of this opposition. For the most part the votes on vital measures of foreign policy left him with more than a merely comfortable margin, and in some instances, notably the Destroyer Deal and Lend Lease, the crippling opposition he so much dreaded never materialized at all. Such fears as the President suffered from appear to have been inspired largely by his antagonists on "the Hill." . . .

In the small hours of Friday morning, September 1, 1939, the President was awakened by a telephone call from Ambassador Bullitt in Paris, informing him that the German armies had just crossed the frontiers of Poland. A few hours later Americans everywhere were listening to the sobering news over their radios, or reading it in their morning newspapers. Apart from a few Communists, and even fewer Nazi sympathizers, the nation was united as rarely before when confronted by shattering events abroad. Sympathy and admiration for Poland were universal.

Nearly everyone held Adolf Hitler responsible for the catastrophe which had now occurred. Hope was therefore general that Britain and France would fulfill their obligations to the Poles, and that together the Allies would defeat the Germans, the more so since the public at large could not wholly suppress the nagging suspicion that any other outcome might conceivably force the United States itself into eventual participation.[1] As to the nation itself entering the conflict at once, American opinion was extraordinarily united. Everything possible, it was agreed, should be done to keep the nation out of war. A poll taken during the first weeks of hostilities confirmed the vitality of this conviction, although, significantly, 44 percent of those consulted already thought American armies should be sent to European battlefields if it appeared that Britain and France were in danger of being defeated. Our national sympathies, then, were crystal clear. We were not really blind to the grave implications for ourselves of the German invasion of Poland; nevertheless, we steadfastly shrank from facing the issues. For the time being, at least, Americans remained determined to steer clear of foreign quarrels, which they had been thoroughly conditioned to suspect and condemn ever since the end of the last war.[2]

---

[1] The most recent public opinion polls (late August) had indicated that 76 percent of those queried professed to believe that the United States was likely to be drawn into a great war. Sixty-one percent favored an economic boycott of dictators who resorted to arms.

[2] The above statement scarcely requires specific documentation, but see the contemporary review in D. F. Fleming: "America Faces the Issue" *(Events,* October 1939, 264–70), and the digests of opinion in the *New York Post,* September 4, and in *The New York Times,* September 8, 10, 1939. For subsequent and more penetrating appraisals of public sentiment see John Crosby Brown: "American Isolation: Propaganda Pro and Con" *(Foreign Affairs,* October 1939), and Raoul de Roussy de Sales: "America Looks at the War" *(Atlantic Monthly,* February 1910).

Despite the strong inference of a friendly biographer that Mr. Roosevelt became convinced when the Hitler-Stalin pact was signed that this nation would be obliged eventually to enter the war, the present authors doubt whether, in the light of so much contrary evidence, the inference can be accepted as more than a natural but passing expression of anxiety.[3] In general they believe that the President shared the attitudes prevalent in the nation, though he and his advisers were naturally better informed than the public at large. Moreover, Mr. Roosevelt was certainly more keenly aware than most of his fellow countrymen of this nation's stake in the conflict which now began to engulf Europe. His aversion to Hitler and his associates was second to none. His hopes for a victory of the democracies were as lively, if by no means as sure, as those of most Americans. Such sentiments were significantly illustrated by the moves the President made just before, as well as just after, the receipt of Ambassador Bullitt's announcement. In order to prevent the great German liner *Bremen* from eluding her British pursuers in her dash for home and safety, he gave instructions that she was to be held at her New York dock on one pretext or another for a minimum of forty-eight hours.[4] Similarly he gave much thought during the final days of August to ways and means by which even after the impend-

ing invocation of the Neutrality Act it might still be possible to transfer certain types of war supplies to the friendly nations without violating the letter of the law.[5] For the rest, the President, according to Assistant Secretary Berle, wanted to postpone issuing the required neutrality proclamation as long as possible, and remarked as early as August 26 that "now is the time to shoot the gun towards getting our neutrality laws changed.[6]

The first shot was actually fired by Assistant Secretary of War Louis Johnson in Boston on August 28, with a speech which, though approved by the President, was more notable for forcefulness than for tact.

If there is much, then, to establish the fact that the President emphatically shared the national desire to assist Britain and France by every safe expedient, there is equally valid evidence that he recoiled from the prospect of war, was determined to spare no effort to keep this nation out of it, and devoutly hoped that by one means or another he would succeed. Thus, at the Cabinet meeting held on the afternoon of September 1, Mr. Roosevelt, in a remarkably somber mood, coupled his intention of summoning a special session of Congress to repeal the arms embargo with expressions of confidence that America would keep out of the war. He recalled the similarity between the current crisis and the hectic hours when the United States entered the First World War. His great concern with measures to prevent economic dislocation and high prices, as well as proposals for discouraging profiteers, "those jackals of war," suggest not merely how closely he shared popular hopes of continued peace, but even how far he was

[3] Alden Hatch: *Franklin D. Roosevelt* (London, 1947), Foreword and pp. 250 ff. Even Professor Beard in his *President Roosevelt and the Coming of the War* (New Haven, 1948. 414 f., admits that Mr. Hatch's statement will be "discounted by critics" unless "supported by authentic documents." We have been unable to find either supporting documents or supporting opinions among those close to the President at this stage.
[4] *Morgenthau Diaries (MS.).* Vol. 206 (August 28, 1939). The flustered port officials managed to carry out orders even though this involved holding up the *Normandie* to save appearances.

[5] Memo describing the Cabinet meeting of August 25, 1939 (*Morgenthau Diaries MS.,* Vol. 206).
[6] *Berle Diaries (MS.),* August 26, 1939; *Moffat Diary (MS.),* September 1, 2, 3, 5, 1939.

himself the victim of popular prejudices against the "munitions makers."[7] . . .

For fully ten days before the conclusion of the destroyers-bases deal [with Britain,] a pall of silence had fallen over Washington. Nothing was given out about the negotiations, and the newspapers, for want of better explanations, began to express impatience over what they assumed must be legalistic hairsplitting. The *Chicago Daily News,* in an editorial of August 22, 1940, warned the administration:

To the average American this business of quibbling over fine points of international law in the face of one of history's gravest threats to all law is a piece of inexcusable stupidity. . . . If Hitler crushes Britain, we can pass laws by the bucketful, without diminishing in any wise the threat to our security.

On the following day the *Christian Science Monitor* wrote: "Those versed in international law can argue the technicalities as long as they like. We believe the ordinary citizen only wants to know whether such sale would put the United States into war." The answer, it thought, was definitely no, since the last thing desired by the Nazis was to bring us into the conflict. Therefore, "the surest way to make international law mean something is to help stop the anarchy produced by those who recognize no law but force."

When at last the news of the deal broke, the general reaction was enthusiastic, the more so as the President in his message to Congress and in his press conference declared the agreement "not inconsistent in any sense with our status of peace. Still less is it a threat against any nation. It is an epochal and far-reaching act of preparation for continental defense in face of grave danger." It was, he asserted, "probably the most important thing that has come for American defense since the Louisiana Purchase." Attorney General Jackson's opinion was also published, in explanation of the President's procedure and to quiet doubts about the legal aspects of the transaction. But little interest was shown in technicalities. The general public, delighted to secure such valuable bases, considered the deal an admirable bargain, even if it seemed to involve something like an Anglo-American alliance. According to the *Christian Science Monitor* (September 4, 1940), "history may record September 2, 1940, as the beginning of the ebb of the totalitarian tide. This trade gives notice that the democracies have the courage and foresight to help each other effectively." Or, to quote the *New York Herald Tribune* (September 4, 1940), "there is no question whatever about the indissoluble link that binds the United States to the fate of the British Isles and the Royal Navy." The deal, it concluded, gave the United States "a stockade of steel to the East."[8]

The terms of the agreement were so exceptionally favorable to the United States that there was initially little disposition in Congress to criticize it or even to question the President's by-passing of the Legislature by resort to the method of executive

---

[7] Hull: *Memoirs,* I, 674 f. We have also used Secretary of the Navy Edison's recollections of the President's remarks at this meeting (*F.D.R.: His Personal Letters, 1928–1945,* II, 915–17), and a memo of Carlton Savage describing the meeting of the State Department on the morning of September 1, 1939, referred to by Mr. Hull. Alsop and Kintner in their *Postscript* to the *American White Paper* (New York, 1940). p. 82a, assert that the alternatives which governed the Administration's choices of policy at the outbreak of the war did not include the possibility of a complete German victory.

[8] On public opinion generally see the country-wide survey of *The New York Times,* September 1, 1940. We have used also an unpublished memorandum of the Council on Foreign Relations entitled *Survey of American Attitudes Towards the War and Its Relation to the United States* (September, 1940).

agreement.[9] To be sure, some effort was made to mobilize opinion against "the dictator." The *St. Louis Post-Dispatch* ran a full-page advertisement in *The New York Times* and other papers (September 4, 1940) sounding the call:

Mr. Roosevelt today committed an act of war. He also became America's first dictator. Secretly his Secretary of State, Mr. Hull, entered into an agreement with the British Ambassador that amounts to a military and naval alliance with Great Britain. . . . The President has passed down an edict that compares with the edicts forced down the throats of Germans, Italians and Russians by Hitler, Mussolini and Stalin. He hands down an edict that may eventually result in the shedding of the blood of millions of Americans; that may result in transforming the United States into a goose-stepping regimented slave-state. . . . Of all sucker real estate deals in history, this is the worst, and the President of the United States is the sucker.

But such truculent attacks evoked little sympathy. When Mr. Willkie rather mildly expressed regret that the President "did not deem it necessary in connection with this proposal to secure the approval of Congress or permit public discussion prior to adoption," his friend, William Allen White, rejoined in public: "When you're negotiating a horse trade, you can't take all the neighbors into confidence." That simple proposition made sense to most Americans.[10]

The position of the isolationists was sadly weakened by their long and well publicized campaign in favor of acquiring bases in the American possessions of the European powers. They would have preferred the purchase of British islands through cancellation of war debts and there was, in fact, some criticism of leasing the facilities instead of securing undisputed sovereignty over them. But in the large even the great isolationist newspapers rejoiced that bases had been obtained and showed little disposition to make an issue of the form of transaction. In the words of one unnamed Senator:

Listen, you can't attack a deal like that. If you jump on the destroyer transfer, you're jumping on the acquisition of defense bases in the Western Hemisphere. And the voters wouldn't stand for that. Roosevelt outsmarted all of us when he tied up the two deals.[11]

So nothing came of the anticipated explosion in the Senate, beyond a bit of surprisingly unimpressive criticism. Senator Nye, as might have been expected, denounced the whole business in advance as "a belligerent act making us a party to the war," and Senator Clark, after roundly attacking the Committee to Defend America and kindred groups which, he asserted with some justice, had rigged the whole deal, quoted with approval the dictum of the *New York Daily News:* "The United States has one foot in the war and the other on a banana peel."[12] But none of this amounted to much and the President had little to worry about. According to the newspapers, Congressional leaders assured him almost at once that the Legislature would take no action in response to his message announcing the agreement.[13] . . .

From the standpoint of both friend and foe . . . the destroyer deal was a milestone

[9] See the summary in *The New York Times,* September 4, 1940, and the *Congressional Digest,* January, 1941, 17 ff.
[10] *The New York Times,* September 4, 1940. On September 6, Willkie, however, reiterated his objection: "Leaving out of account the advantage or disadvantage of the trade, the method by which that trade was effected was the most arbitrary and dictatorial action ever taken by any President in the history of the United States" (*The New York Times,* September 7, 1940).
[11] *New York Post,* September 9, 1940.
[12] *The New York Times,* September 2, 1940; *Congressional Record,* September 26, 1940.
[13] *The New York Times,* September 5, 1940.

in the development of American policy. The United States had obviously abandoned neutrality and, though Americans refused to recognize the new-fangled Fascist term "nonbelligerency," had entered upon a status of "limited war." Mr. Churchill, in his great address of August 20, 1940, had predicted that the transaction would mean that Britain and the United States would become "somewhat mixed up together in some of their affairs for mutual and general advantage." It was a process, he said, that he viewed without misgiving and which, as we know, he accepted gladly as being inevitable: "I could not stop it if I wished; no one can stop it. Like the Mississippi, it just keeps rolling along."

The historian can hardly challenge the Prime Minister's interpretation, even though it originated in a time of intense crisis and reflected a highly partisan approach. For the events of the years 1938 to 1940 had taught the American people not only the dangers of Nazi aggression but also the larger community of interest that bound the democracies to each other. In September, 1940, Americans were still hoping against hope that by large scale aid to Britain they could avoid military participation in the war. But the old isolationism was now almost dead and few Americans subscribed to anything more than what might be called noninterventionism. The country had come to recognize its stake in the survival and ultimate victory of Britain, and it could already be predicted with considerable confidence that in the future, American policy would proceed, though reluctantly and regretfully, to any lengths required for the defeat of Hitler and his allies.

This fundamental development, it should be noted, was the expression of the popular understanding and the popular will. Those who would lay the responsibility at the door of the President will find little support in the story of the destroyer deal, for throughout the summer it was the President who held back. In the beginning he was understandably loath to part with any weapons useful for self-defense and was probably somewhat suspicious of British intentions. Later on he showed himself fearful of Congress and apprehensive lest his Republican opponent exploit the transaction. The President's secretary, Miss Tully, has recorded that Mr. Roosevelt, while drafting his message to Congress in late August, remarked: "Congress is going to raise hell about this, but even another day's delay may mean the end of civilization. Cries of 'warmonger' and 'dictator' will fill the air, but if Britain is to survive, we must act."[14] While conceding that it took courage to embark upon so grave a transaction on the eve of a national election, one must recognize that Mr. Roosevelt's way had been carefully prepared by those organizations which not only plotted a safe course for him but also carried the burden of public education. The destroyer deal was at least as much the achievement of private effort as of official action and it should be viewed as a truly popular, national commitment to share in the conflict against Hitler to the extent required by American security.

* * *

The majority which in midsummer [1940] had thought it more important to assist Britain than to avoid war was by autumn again tending to diminish in size. By October's end the American people were probably about evenly divided on the wisdom of taking this risk. The momentary cessation of spectacular action on European battlefields after the Battle of Britain evidently produced a rapid increase in the

---

[14] Grace Tully: *FDR: My Boss*, 244.

number of those who felt that somehow, after all, the British would win.[15]

Opinion on the issue of aid to Britain in the pre-election weeks may therefore be described as firm at the two extremes and fluid in the middle. At one extreme was a small, vocal, and determined minority, including many influential citizens, who favored an outright alliance with Britain. They urged supplying money, materials, and, if necessary, men. They were prepared to face a war if this program rendered war inevitable. At the other extreme was a still smaller minority of diehard isolationists, together with a scattering of pro-Nazis and pro-Communists, who were for ending at once assistance to Britain of any description whatsoever.

In between these two extremes, and comprising roughly three quarters of the American people, was a mass of opinion favoring at the very least no significant diminution in the prevailing scale of American aid to Britain and, indeed, advocating on the whole any increase in such assistance as could safely be contemplated without involving the United States itself in hostilities. But when confronted with the point-blank question of whether or not to go to war now, American opinion was still overwhelmingly in favor of remaining out.[16]

Behind these evidences of profound indecision with which Americans were confronting the issue of aid to the democracies remained two deeply ingrained popular sentiments. One was the natural desire to avoid war if possible or, at least, as long as possible. The other was the fatalistic assumption that, willy-nilly, the United States would find itself in the war before the conflict ended. Perhaps, therefore, the sooner the better. . . .

In his acceptance speech to the Democratic Convention on July 19, 1940 the President had warned his audience and the nation that he was going to undertake no personal campaigning. He would stand on his record and would intervene in the campaign only if he were confronted by "deliberate or unwitting falsification of fact." With his superior sense of timing, the President refrained from justifying his foreign and defense policies before the electorate from July 19 until October 23, 1940. . . .

Mr. Roosevelt delivered the first of . . . five addresses at Philadelphia on October 23, the day after Mr. [Wendell] Willkie, speaking in Chicago, had again derisively challenged the good faith of his opponent's assurances that he would keep the country out of war. The Philadelphia speech was an effective piece of campaigning, but it ended abruptly any faint hope that Mr. Roosevelt's long-postponed rebuttal would illuminate the major issues of foreign policy. Asserting that his rival's constant re-iteration of untrue charges against the Administration resembled the Nazi propaganda technique of repeating lies so consistently that they came to be accepted as truth, the President branded as complete falsehood the allegation that he had entered into secret commitments with foreign nations which endangered the national security or pledged the United States Government to participate in the war:

I give to you and to the people of this country this most solemn assurance: There is no secret treaty, no secret obligation, no secret understanding in any shape or form, direct or indirect, with any other Government or any other nation in any part of the world, to involve this nation in any war or for any other purpose.[17]

[15] *Public Opinion Quarterly,* March, 1941, pp. 158 ff.

[16] *Ibid.,* p. 159. In mid-October a poll indicated 83 percent of Americans registering "no" in response to the question whether the United States should enter the war against Germany and Italy at once.

[17] *Public Papers and Addresses,* IX, 485 ff.

The reader may judge from the record, so far as the authors have been able to reconstruct it, the President's veracity in making this statement. Having forcefully made it, Mr. Roosevelt devoted most of the Philadelphia speech to domestic political issues. However, before finishing he took occasion to denounce as another Republican falsification the charge that he wished to lead the country into war. Asserting that on this point he stood firmly on the plank of the Democratic Party's platform (repeating it word for word), the President ended with the words: "It is for peace that I have labored; and it is for peace that I shall labor all the days of my life."

In view of the abundant evidence supporting Mr. Roosevelt's assertion of his abhorrence of war and his anxiety to maintain peace, provided peace was compatible with the national security, it was fitting that he should have repudiated the oft-repeated imputation that he deliberately courted war. But this was scarcely the essence of the issue. Insofar as Mr. Willkie's charges had any validity, they reduced themselves to the accusation that the methods the President used to carry out his foreign policy, and particularly the scope of the program for assisting Britain by all means short of war, involved the evident risk of ultimate American involvement in the hostilities. On this, the crucial issue, Mr. Roosevelt had nothing to say to the American people at Philadelphia or anywhere else.

It would be monotonous to recount in detail the charges and countercharges which the two rivals exchanged day by day, almost hour by hour in the final stage of the campaign. Wendell Willkie, having long since exhausted his substantial themes, abandoned the last vestiges of restraint in denouncing the good faith of his opponent. He recklessly invited those of his fellow citizens who regarded the survival of Britain as absolutely vital to American security, as well as those who were certain that peace for the Americas was the supreme objective of American policy, to unite on him as President. He left no lingering suspicion in the minds of his audience that he might conceivably fail to achieve both these objectives concurrently. The Republican nominee reached his climax at Baltimore on October 30, when he told his audience that if the President were re-elected, "you may expect we will be at war." [18]

The President, who had replied in kind to each challenge offered by his opponent, was speaking in Boston on the same day that Mr. Willkie spoke at Baltimore.... He had, to the great satisfaction of his professional advisers on foreign policy, determined to make the Boston speech the occasion for informing the American people of his decision to permit the British Government to place billions of dollars' worth of new munitions orders in the United States. This announcement was to incorporate the wording agreed upon in advance by the appropriate members of his Cabinet and by the British as well. By clear implication, therefore, Mr. Roosevelt would publicly commit the United States to a program of aid to Britain which could with difficulty be reconciled with positive assurance that the United States would not engage in foreign wars.

Moreover, other minds than those of Messrs. Hull, Morgenthau, Stimson and Knox were to have a part in the drafting of the President's Boston address. The party politicians were now importuning Mr. Roosevelt. If he did not once and for all give a categorical promise to the electorate that America's young men would not be sent to fight in foreign wars if he were

---

[18] *The New York Times*, October 31, 1940.

re-elected, the election was lost. This urgent plea was dinned into the President's ears even on the train to Boston. Mr. Roosevelt at first objected strenuously to the inclusion of any such promise in the text of his speech. What, he asked, is a foreign war? Does it mean we will fight only in a civil war? In the end, however, convincing himself that the proposed phraseology was sufficiently obscure and meaningless, he consented to insert it as the only sure antidote to Willkie's poison about American boys being already on the transports.[19]

Accordingly, at Boston, on the night of October 30, 1940, the President capped Mr. Willkie's climax with words which, if they seemed meaningless to him, doubtless seemed sufficiently clear to his nationwide audience:

> And while I am talking to you mothers and fathers I give you one more assurance.
>
> I have said this before, but I shall say it again and again and again:
>
> Your boys are not going to be sent into any foreign wars.
>
> They are going into training to form a force so strong that, by its very existence, it will keep the threat of war far away from our shores.
>
> The purpose of our defense is defense.[20]

This was indeed categorical assurance to the American people, beside which the President's subsequent reference to the vast program of aid to Britain scarcely seemed to the man in the street a significant qualification. Nothing that Mr. Roosevelt was to say from then until Election Day approached the forcefulness of this unqualified commitment to the American people. The "Champ" had decisively outplayed Willkie at the latter's own game. There would be leisure to repent that in resorting to devices against which

his own sound political instinct rebelled, the Chief Executive seriously weakened the cause he sought to advance and added no luster to his reputation for sincerity....

These campaign pronouncements constitute a reasonable sample of the quality of the debate through which the American people were supposed to resolve the mental confusion which had made it so easy for them simultaneously to advocate increased aid to Britain and avoidance of war. In effect, the only conclusion the voters were logically entitled to draw from the campaign of 1940 was their right, on the very highest authority, to persist in incompatible courses of action....

Could the President, mindful of the campaign pledges he had made, notably at Boston, really regard his re-election as the mandate he needed to chart American policy along the course he thought necessary to insure the national security?[21] Within certain limits the answer was certainly in the affirmative. Mr. Roosevelt felt safe in announcing on November 8 that henceforth the Administration would apply a fifty-fifty "rule of thumb" in dividing munitions production with Great Britain. Various concrete measures of aid to Britain, held in escrow during the final weeks of the campaign, were ... quickly released at the signal of the President's re-election.

Nevertheless, if Mr. Roosevelt could and did assume that the mandate of the people provided clear endorsement of what he had done for Britain since the previous spring, there could be no assurance that it could be stretched to cover the far riskier measures which he well knew would have to be undertaken in the near future if Britain's resistance was to be sustained. This was the price he had to pay for his belief,

---

[19] Conversation of the authors with Mr. Robert E. Sherwood (who helped to write this speech), April, 1948; Sherwood: *Roosevelt and Hopkins*, 190–92.
[20] *Public Papers and Addresses*, IX, 514 ff.

[21] On this point see the President's own analysis in letters to King George VI and to Mr. Samuel I. Rosenman *(F.D.R.: His Personal Letters*, II, 1078 ff., 1083 ff.). Cf. Sherwood: *Roosevelt and Hopkins*, 200 ff.

right or wrong, that to plead the case for his foreign policy in a manner calculated to produce clarification rather than confusion in the public mind would have cost him the 1940 election.

Be that as it may, Mr. Roosevelt's decision to leave the edges of his future intentions blurred entailed serious disadvantages. It laid him open to the charge, which the present authors believe unfounded, that he was deliberately misleading the American public by holding out promises of peace while actually plotting measures to lead the nation into war. It placed a brake on many measures which he really believed urgently necessary to bolster Britain's position. It prolonged unduly the slow tempo of American rearmament. Most of all, it permitted the American people yet a while to cherish the agreeable illusion that they could both eat their cake and have it.

The first scholarly work on Japanese-American relations before 1942 was *The Road to Pearl Harbor* (1950) by HERBERT FEIS (b. 1893). A member of the State Department for several years, Feis had a wide circle of acquaintances in the Roosevelt Administration who granted him access to important source materials for his study. Because of this and because of its sympathetic portrayal of the Roosevelt Administration's policies, Feis's volume has sometimes been labeled an "official history." It has also been described as a balanced work of scholarship based on careful research in the sources. Which of these conclusions is more persuasive?*

Herbert Feis

American Policy Restrained and Realistic

There was no plan in the autumn of 1939 to use sanctions against Japan. There was a state of mind, becoming more confirmed, which forbade compromise with Japan. Sooner or later, states of mind express themselves in action. After the treaty [of commerce] was cancelled [in July, 1939,] anything might happen. [Ambassador Joseph] Grew wanted the American government to divert the indicated course of events by again seeking a settlement with Japan; and, as a way of showing its wish to remain friends, to propose some temporary substitute for the treaty. Another entry in his diary at this time summarizes his affirmations:

I believe that we should now offer the Japanese a *modus vivendi*, in effect if not in name, that

we shall commence negotiations for a new treaty, withholding ratification until favorable developments appear to justify. . . .

In my view the use of force, except in defense of a nation's sovereignty, can only constitute admission of a lack of good will and of resourceful, imaginative statesmanship. To those who hold that it is not enough for these qualities to exist on one side—my answer is that they do exist in latent form in Japan and the function of diplomacy is to bring them into vigor. Shidehara [or conciliatory] diplomacy has existed. It can exist again.

The President and Secretary of State shared the hope expressed in the final sentence of this entry. But where were the reasons for the belief that this change could be effected by a mere show of patience and good will, as Grew seemed to think? While they had the treaty, Japanese governments had not valued it enough to listen to us. Why would they begin to do so now—if the treaty were restored? Both the President and Hull wanted prior proofs of a change in aims and methods. Grew's idea was rejected. He was told, instead, to speak out . . . [in] Japan in a way that would bring home to both the government and people of that country that trouble was ahead unless they changed their policies.

The text of the speech in which this was to be said received much study within the State Department. It was to be resonant but not threatening. Grew reconciled himself with the thought that if American policy was not to conform to his ideas, it was best, anyhow, that Japan be plainly told what it was to be. In that way, at least, the risk of war through ignorant misjudgment might be lessened.

Grew delivered his notice that the American government would not back down, and that, therefore, if trouble was to be avoided the Japanese Army must. During the weeks that followed, it seemed to the American government to be having some measure of effect. There were signs—which proved to be passing—that the Japanese government might deal less harshly with American interests and activities in China; the Japanese government promised to reopen the Yangtze River to foreign traffic. But these small acts of care were offset by the efforts to create a puppet Chinese government in Nanking and thereby to disavow Chiang Kai-shek's group as the legal government of China. Washington called the new regime by its true name and refused to recognize it. The warning spoken by Grew, it appeared, would be defied.

But Hull still paused. Opinion was divided and uncertain. On November 6 [1939] Senator [Key] Pittman predicted

the Congress would authorize the use of economic pressure on Japan. Senator [Arthur] Vandenberg contradicted him at once, warning that such threats were the first step towards war itself.

Anything of that sort that was done would have to be done alone. Compelled to fight their own battle in Europe, neither Britain nor France wanted trouble in the Far East. If it should become necessary to protect their own position in that region, they were ready to compromise with Japan. As explained by Lord Lothian, the British Ambassador (on November 21 and subsequently), his government favored some accord between China and Japan "on a basis which would be fair and equitable to both sides, but with the realization on the part of both China and Japan that each side would have to make concessions." The French government leaned the same way.

But the American bent stiffly the other way. Thus [Sumner] Welles, then Acting Secretary, told Lothian that the American government could not and would not do anything to bring pressure on China to make a peace which was not just or which assigned a preferential place to Japan in China. Hull lectured Lothian in the same sense, on December 15. The American government, he asserted, had done its utmost to bring about a fair settlement in the Far East; but in his view Japan was bent on turning the whole of China into a vast Manchukuo [Japan's Manchurian puppet state]; the American government could not consider such a policy and would not depart from the position and principles which it had been defending since first Japan began its conquest of Asia.

The British and French authorities bowed to our judgment, but with a reminder that if it were wrong the first blows would hit them and not us. They remained uneasy. So did Grew. He resumed his efforts to make sure that the American government did not enter into, fall into, the error of thinking that Japan would yield to pressure. Thus, in a long and considered dispatch sent on December 1, he wrote in part:

On one issue [Japanese] opinion can be definitely said to be unanimous: the so-called New Order in East Asia has come to stay. That term is open to wide interpretation, but the minimum interpretation envisages permanent Japanese control of Manchuria, Inner Mongolia, and North China.

Sanctions, he was sure, would not cause Japan to give up its program in China, but would arouse it to fight—since it was a nation of hardy warriors, with an ingrained spirit to do or die.

This estimate agreed on the whole with that made within the State Department. But Grew's advice did not seem to jibe with it, but rather to issue from some do-or-die professional instinct of his own. How or why diplomacy could win the day, if Japan was so hard set upon the creation of a new order throughout Asia, remained unclear. Hull decided that the best course for the time being was merely to prolong the uncertainty. To refrain from the use of sanctions which might produce a crisis, but also to refuse to give Japan any guarantee as to what the United States might do in the future. On December 14 the President approved this course.

Grew, as expected, questioned the decision. So did the British and French. Hull's answer to Grew, on December 20, stated that while he also desired to give the . . . [Japanese] Cabinet every chance to increase its influence over the Army, he had the impression that at the bottom it was as keen as the Army to extend Japanese power over Asia. Though more prudent, perhaps, because better informed of the risks, it was hardly less ambitious. To

Lothian (on December 15) he repeated that the United States could not consider any policy that would enable Japan to achieve a victorious peace.

By the turn of the new year, 1940, it was settled that we would neither renew nor replace the treaty. The United States kept itself free to end at any time the shipment of goods vital to Japan. When told of this decision, Nomura, the Foreign Minister, was bitter and depressed. For the first time, Grew noticed, he did not accompany him downstairs after their talk.

But no crisis was to be forced. Trade with Japan was to be allowed to go on in much the same way as when the treaty was in force. Japan was left unhindered to win or lose the battle in China; to scheme for a southern empire or renounce the dream. . . .

On September 19 [1940] after hearing about the latest Japanese ultimatum to Indo-China [about military facilities in the northern provinces], the President and cabinet agreed that the time had come to put a total stop to the export of scrap iron and steel. The defense agencies were getting out of hand in their opinion that the country should not export any more—except to Britain. Hull, as the news came in day by day of the fighting over England, grew less worried about what Japan might do. On the heels of this decision word came from Grew that the Japanese government had decided on some form of alliance with Germany; that on the previous day the matter had been settled in a three-hour conference in the presence of the Emperor.

Still it was judged best to wait until Japanese armies had actually marched into Indo-China. By the 24th [of September] they had, and reports of the projected alliance with Germany became confirmed. In haste another loan to China was arranged; and on the 25th it was announced. The next day the President ordered that the export of all grades of iron and steel scrap be placed under control. Without contradiction the press wrote that there was to be an "embargo." This time the statement stood.

Of oil nothing was said. Some might argue that the ending of exports of that most vital product would stop Japan and avert war. Hull and the Navy did not believe it. Nor did the British or the Dutch.

The scrap embargo was both a reproof and a penalty. One which had practical effect in the scales of war strength, and as such a signal that the United States thought it might get into war with Japan. In retrospect it was . . . a crossing of the bridge from words to deeds. But even so, the measure brought only thin satisfaction to many in Washington. They thought it both little and too late. If the ban imposed in September had included oil, if it had been taken earlier, they thought that Japan would not have dared attack Indo-China, or enter into an alliance with Germany and Italy. [Secretary of the Treasury] Morgenthau [Secretary of War] Stimson, and [Secretary of the Interior] Ickes were among those of that view. As expressed in an entry in Morgenthau's diary on September 23:

My own opinion is that the time to put pressure on Japan was before she went into Indo-China and not after and I think it's too late and I think the Japanese and the rest of the dictators are just going to laugh at us. The time to have done it was months ago and then maybe Japan would have stopped, looked and listened.

As to that, who is to know? But after study of the Japanese records, I think this a mirage. Had Hull not waited upon evidence that Britain would hold out, and had the President not borne with him, all our

history might have been different. My own best surmise is that stronger and earlier action would not have caused Japan to slow up, then desist from its course. More probably, I think, it would have caused it to move farther and faster. The Indo-Chinese expedition would probably not have stopped in the north. The terms of alliance with the Axis might well have been more clinching. Not improbably, Japan, despite the reluctance of its Navy, would have ceased to dally with the Indies. Or, in the coming January, when Hitler was greatly to want Japan to move against Singapore, it would have done so. In either event, the crisis in the Pacific might well have come during the winter of 1940–41, instead of the next one.

Such, rather than peace in the Pacific would have been, I think, the outcome of an earlier application of compelling sanctions. Unless, unless the United States had been willing (and sufficiently united in sentiment) at the same time to send the Pacific Fleet to Singapore, to make known that it would join Britain, France, and Holland in the defense of their Far Eastern possessions. That might have worked. If it had not, the United States would have been at war. But in all this I have let conjecture go free and far, and the opinions ventured are without benefit of notary or proof of legitimacy. . . .

November 1940; the Roosevelt administration was safely confirmed in power. It could properly construe the election result as approval of its opposition to the Axis and its support of Britain short of war. But, because of the terms in which he had expounded these policies during the campaign, the President was obliged still to move warily and on the slant. The words spoken during the election contest lived on to complicate and confine decision for the times ahead.

Americans had been told that they need
not take part in the battles then being
fought in Europe and Asia and that the
government would not cause them to do
so. They had been urged to provide weapons and resources to fend off the danger of
having to go to war. British resistance, the
expressed thought ran, was giving us time
to become so strong that no country, or
group of countries, would dare attack us.
While if the Axis won, the United States
would become exposed to its fury and
forced to fight near or within our own
land. This was a correct judgment of the
meaning to us of the wars in Europe and
Asia. It was a well founded basis for the
program sponsored by the government and
for the acceptance of the connected risks.
But it left the President open to a charge
of blunder or bad faith if the United States
found itself at war.

The government avoided all actions
which could not be construed as defensive.
It continued—and it was no easy thing to
do—to refuse to enter into any accord
which carried an obligation to go to war.
But it shaped our policies in conference
with other governments and fitted its action to theirs. We were about to form a
common front against Japan without ad-
mitting it or promising to maintain it by
force. . . .

The world may long wonder what
would have happened had the President
agreed then [in September, 1941] to meet
with [Premier] Konoye. Grew and [Coun-
selor of Embassy, Eugene] Dooman, at the
time and later, had a sense that the refusal
was a sad error. To them it seemed that
the American government missed a real
chance to lead Japan back to peaceful
ways. Konoye, they thought, was sincere in
his acceptance of those principles of international conduct for which the American
government stood, and with the support of
the Emperor would be able to carry

through his promises. In words which
Grew confided to his diary:

It is my belief that the Emperor, the Government of Prince Konoye and the militant leaders
of Japan (the leaders then in control) had come
to accept the status of the conflict in China, in
conjunction with our freezing measures and
Japan's economic condition as evidence of failure or comparative incapacity to succeed.

Our attitude, he thought (and others
since have thought the same), showed a
lack both of insight and suppleness, if not
of desire. The mistake sprang, in this view,
from failure to appreciate why Konoye
could not be as clear and conclusive as the
American government wished; and to admit that Japan could correct its course
only in a gradual and orderly way. Wise
American statesmanship, thus, would have
bartered adjustment for adjustment,
agreeing to relax our economic restraints
little by little as Japan, little by little, went
our way. Instead, the judgment ends, it
was dull and inflexible. By insisting that
Japan promise in black and white, then
and there, to conform to every American
requirement, it made Konoye's task impossible.

It will be always possible to think that
Grew was correct; that the authorities in
Washington were too close to their texts
and too soaked in their disbelief to perceive what he saw. That the American government was as stern as a righteous
schoolmaster cannot be denied. Nor that it
was unwilling either to ease Japanese failure, or to provide any quick or easy way
to improve their hard lot. But the records
since come to hand do not support the belief that a real chance of maintaining
peace in the Pacific—on or close to the
terms for which we had stood since 1931—
was missed. They do not confirm the opinion that Konoye was prepared, without
reserve or trickery, to observe the rules set
down by Hull. Nor that he would have

been able to do so, even though a respite was granted and he was allowed to grade the retreat gently.

If Konoye was ready and able—as Grew thought—to give Roosevelt trustworthy and satisfactory promises of a new sort, he does not tell of them in his "Memoirs." Nor has any other record available to me disclosed them. He was a prisoner, willing or unwilling, of the terms precisely prescribed in conferences over which he presided. The latest of these were the minimum demands specified by the Imperial Conference of September 6 [1941]. . . . It is unlikely that he could have got around them or that he would have in some desperate act discarded them. The whole of his political career speaks to the contrary.

In proof of his ability to carry out his assurances, Konoye stressed first, that his ideas were approved by the Army and Navy; and second, that senior officials (Vice-Chiefs of Staff) of both branches would accompany him on his mission. If and when he said "Yes," they would say "Yes"; and thus the United States could count upon unified execution of any accord. But it seems to me far more likely that the Army and Navy had other thoughts in mind on assigning high officials to go along with him. They would be there to see that Konoye did not yield to the wish for peace or the will of the President. The truer version of the bond is expressed in the title of one of the sub-sections of Konoye's "Memoirs": "The Independence of the Supreme Command and State Affairs from Each Other: The Anguish of Cabinets from Generation to Generation."

Konoye could have honestly agreed that Japan would stop its southern advance and reduce its forces in China to the minimum needed to assure compliance with its wishes. That is really all. To the seekers of the New Order in East Asia this seemed much; to the American government it

seemed too little. The error, the fault, in American policy—if there was one—was not in the refusal to trust what Konoye could honestly offer. It was in insisting that Japan entirely clear out of Indo-China and China (and perhaps out of Manchukuo) and give up all exclusive privileges in these countries.

In any case, the President and Hull were convinced that Konoye's purposes were murky and his freedom of decision small. Therefore they concluded that to meet with him before Japan proved its intentions would be a great mistake. It could bring confusion into both American policies and our relations with the other opponents of the Axis. So Grew's earnest appeal for a daring try did not influence the responses to Japan that Hull's drafting squad was putting together. They took nothing that came from Tokyo for granted; wanted everything shown. The Army and Navy were both saying that they could use well all the time they could get. Both Stimson and [Secretary of the Navy] Knox approved "stringing out negotiations." But neither wanted Roosevelt to meet Konoye or to soften American terms just to gain time.

Hull was guided by these thoughts in the prepared answer which he gave [Ambassador] Nomura on October 2, the answer on which the plans of Japan hung. The Japanese proposals (of September 6), this said in effect, did not provide a basis for a settlement, and were on essential points ambiguous. The meeting between the President and Konoye was put off till there was a real meeting of minds about . . . the essential foundations of proper relations.

Upon reading this, the opinion nurtured by Konoye and [Foreign Minister] Toyoda, that Japanese and American terms could be reconciled, dropped. This, the note of October 2, rather than the one of November 26 on which controversy has centered, ended the era of talk. For the crisis that followed in Japan brought into power a group determined to fight us rather than move further our way. Thereafter war came first, diplomacy second. . . .

[Ambassador] Kurusu arrived in Washington [on November 16, 1941]. A clipper brought him, and his flight across the Pacific was watched as though he were a bird whose coming could bring fair weather or foul. But the government knew that he was only a trained expositor of matters already decided.

Hull on the 17th introduced him to the President. The ensuing talk was only a snarled survey of the area of dissension. The President did not sprinkle his words with geniality, as he usually had with Nomura. There was no liking either for the man or for his mission. As for the man, Hull spoke for both when he wrote: "Kurusu seemed to me the antithesis of Nomura. Neither his appearance nor his attitude commanded confidence or respect. I felt from the start that he was deceitful." As for the mission, that was unpromising, even if not false. His purpose, looked at in the best light, was to persuade the American government to accept the latest Japanese terms in preference to war. Looked at in the worst light, it was to engage American interest while the assault plans were being secretly completed. Just before the meeting, another cable of warning had been received from Grew. Be on guard, he said, against sudden naval and military actions, for Japan would probably exploit every possible tactical advantage, such as surprise and initiative.

On the next day, the 18th, the talk took an unmapped turn. Nomura, speaking as though the idea were his own, asked whether it might not be possible to arrange a type of accord other than that [Proposal A] over which the two governments were now so completely at odds. Perhaps, he suggested, a partial agreement which

would at least avert immediate trouble. His thought, he said, was that the two governments might restore the situation as it was before July [1941] when Japan moved into Southern Indo-China, and the United States and Britain imposed their embargo.

Hull, up to that point had been ungiving. But here was a chance, at least, to gain time. Time that would fit us (and our associates) better for war. Time that might enable the Japanese government to persuade the Army to yield more, and the people to accept the thought of retreat. As broached, it was only an idea, incomplete and without authority. Hull said just enough to show he was attracted, no more. He asked Nomura whether, if such an arrangement were made, the talks would continue. Nomura said they would. Hull then observed that he could see how this step might enable the Japanese leaders to hold their position and to organize public opinion in favor of a peaceful course. Therefore he would acquaint the British and Dutch governments with the suggestion and see what they thought.

Nomura and Kurusu stood on tiptoe in the effort to put this idea across. That night (November 18) they hurried off message after message to Tokyo. Togo, the Foreign Minister, had sent them some days before the text of Proposal B—terms for a truce to be offered as a last resort. But its rejection was foreseen by them. The two Japanese diplomats were trying to prevent the final crash by proffering easier and simpler truce terms.

As soon as the Japanese had left, Hull asked Sir Ronald Campbell, British Chargé d'Affaires, to call. He told Campbell of the status of the talks and of the idea of a partial arrangement to allow the Japanese government to direct public opinion. On the next morning he spoke to the Chinese Ambassador and the Australian and Dutch Ministers in the same sense and with a certain show of eagerness.

But "Magic" [the ability to read top-priority diplomatic code] brought the news that the notions of the two Ambassadors had been rejected in Tokyo. The Foreign Minister frowned on their flow of advice that Japan should accept a loose "give and take" truce rather than a long drawn-out war. They were told that the Japanese government could not agree to withdraw from Indo-China, merely in return for relaxation of trade controls; that it was afraid that the American government would soon bring up other and further conditions. They were ordered to present at once the whole of Proposal B. . . .

Nomura placed Proposal B before Hull on November 20. The English text, as cabled some days before, had been intercepted and read. Hull knew that it was regarded in Tokyo as the last bargain; the hinge on the breech of the cannon.

There were five numbered points on the white piece of paper which Nomura gave to Hull. They have been printed in many other places, but I think the reader will want them before him as he follows the narrative:

1. Both the Government of Japan and the United States undertake not to make any armed advancement into any of the regions in the South-eastern Asia and the Southern Pacific area excepting the part of French Indo-China where the Japanese troops are stationed at present.
2. The Japanese Government undertakes to withdraw its troops now stationed in French Indo-China upon either the restoration of peace between Japan and China or the establishment of an equitable peace in the Pacific area.

In the meantime the Government of Japan declares that it is prepared to remove its troops now stationed in the southern part of French Indo-China to the northern part of the said territory upon the conclusion of the present arrangement which shall later be embodied in the final agreement.
3. The Government of Japan and the United States shall cooperate with a view to

securing the acquisition of those goods and commodities which the two countries need in Netherlands East Indies.
4. The Government of Japan and the United States mutually undertake to restore their commercial relations to those prevailing prior to the freezing of the assets.

The Government of the United States shall supply Japan a required quantity of oil.
5. The Government of the United States undertakes to refrain from such measures and actions as will be prejudicial to the endeavors for the restoration of general peace between Japan and China.

Whoever insisted on the last paragraph—Tojo and the Army certainly did—insisted on war.

Hull glanced over the text to make sure it was the same as that which was known. It was. Then, on two points in particular he spoke out. Linking Japan's treatment of China to Hitler's actions, he defended our aid to China. Kurusu remarked that perhaps this point (No. 5) in the Japanese terms might be construed to mean that the United States would end its help only at the time when talks between Japan and China would have started. Hull also dwelt on the fact that this truce would leave Japan a full member of the Axis pact, and hence still a potential enemy of the United States and Great Britain. To this Kurusu had no answer.

Hull found no dissent, either within the State Department or at the White House, to his opinion that the proposal was "clearly unacceptable." His reasons for finding it so are summed up again in his "Memoirs":

The commitments we should have to make were virtually a surrender. We on our part should have to supply Japan as much oil as she might require, suspend our freezing measures, and resume full commercial relations with Tokyo. We should have to discontinue aid to China and withdraw our moral and material support from the recognized Chinese Government of Chiang Kai-shek. We should have to help Japan obtain products of the Netherlands East Indies. We should have to cease augmenting our military forces in the western Pacific.

Japan, on her part, would still be free to continue her military operations in China, to attack the Soviet Union, and to keep her troops in northern Indo-China until peace was effected with China ... Japan thus clung to her vantage point in Indo-China which threatened countries to the south and vital trade routes.

The President and I could only conclude that agreeing to these proposals would mean condonement by the United States of Japan's past aggressions, assent to future courses of conquest by Japan, abandonment of the most essential principles of our foreign policy, betrayal of China and Russia, and acceptance of the role of silent partner aiding and abetting Japan in her effort to create a Japanese hegemony over the western Pacific and eastern Asia.

Inspection of such Japanese records as I have seen leaves room for doubt about some features of this judgment. It is not certain that the meaning which Hull attached to some of the points in Proposal B is the necessary meaning; or that his total estimate of the Japanese offer to begin to retreat was just. Perhaps so, probably so, but not surely so.

It would be a barren exercise, I think, now to re-examine, feature by feature, the face and soul of this last Japanese formula for peace. The result would be inconclusive; for even its authors were divided and mixed up in their intentions. And even a less suspicious reading would have, I think, led to the same rejection. For the situation had grown too immense and entangled for haggling. Japan had forced the creation of a defensive coalition more vast than the empire of the Pacific for which it plotted. This was not now to be quieted by a temporary halt along the fringe of the Japanese advance.

Acceptance of this Japanese proposal would have imperilled the trustful unity of the coalition. As the next few days were to show, China would have felt itself deserted, if not betrayed. Elsewhere the will to carry on the fight against Germany without pause or compromise might have been corrupted. The Japanese Army and Navy would have been left in place to take advantage of any future weakness.

Even—to carry conjecture further—if the American government had taken these risks and entered into this accord, there would have been war in the Pacific. For it seems to me almost certain that the truce would have broken down as soon as signed. Quarrels would have started over the military movements in which both sides were engaged. Japan would not have ceased its preparations for attack. Nor can it be thought that we or the British would have ended the movement of planes and ships and anti-aircraft and radar to the Philippines and Malaya. Each side would have thought the other to be taking crooked advantage of the truce.

If these disputes did not bring the truce to a quick end, arguments over oil would have done so. Very different notions existed in Tokyo and Washington as to what was expected under the phrase "a required quantity of oil." The Japanese government had told Nomura to let us know before signing how much it had in mind. It wanted four million tons a year from the United States, and one million tons a year from the Indies. The American government would not have agreed to supply anything like such quantities, which were enough to keep Japanese reserves intact.

In sum, the paper given by Nomura to Hull on November 20 would have marked only the start of new disputes, not the end of old ones.

In the late 1940s and early 1950s a number of writers began challenging the assumption that Japanese aggression was primarily to blame for the war in the Pacific. The historians Charles C. Tansill and Harry Elmer Barnes published books which argued that the Roosevelt Administration provoked the Japanese into an attack on the United States, the ultimate motive being to give the administration a "back door" to the war in Europe. ANTHONY KUBEK (b. 1920), a professor of political science at the University of Dallas, voices and expands upon this thesis in the following selection. Does Kubek persuasively show why and how the Administration led the country into war with Japan?*

Anthony Kubek

American Policy Intentionally Provocative

When Franklin Roosevelt became President in 1933, he supported the "Stimson Doctrine" without reservation. But it was apparent to seasoned diplomats that the manner in which Stimson endeavored to apply the non-recognition formula was so provocative that war with Japan became a possibility. It is significant that during the first Cabinet meeting of the Roosevelt Administration, March 7, 1933, the eventuality of war with Japan was carefully considered. Already the shadows of conflict were beginning to cloud the Far Eastern picture.

On October 5, 1937, the President made a famous address at Chicago, in which he advocated a "quarantine" against aggressor nations. His words of sharp criticism were directed chiefly at Japan, and it is evident that his challenging words marked a tragic turning-point in U. S. relations with Japan. He had inaugurated a new policy of pressure that helped drive Americans down the road to war.

On July 26, 1939, notice was given to Japan that after six months the Commercial Treaty of February 21, 1911 would expire. This action was a blow to the national pride of the Japanese. The big question for the Roosevelt Administration was whether to employ economic sanctions against Japan. Concerning this campaign of economic pressure, Ambassador Joseph C. Grew remarked: "I have pointed out that once started on a policy of sanctions, we must see them through and that such a

*From Anthony Kubek, *How the Far East Was Lost* (Chicago: Henry Regnery Company, 1963), pp. 3–7, 12–24. Footnotes omitted.

policy may conceivably lead to eventual war." However, in order to see sanctions through, Roosevelt brought into his Cabinet on June 20, 1940, as Secretary of War, Henry L. Stimson who had convinced him of the efficacy of that policy back in January, 1933.

With the arrival of Stimson in the Cabinet, the Roosevelt Administration began to forge an economic chain around Japan that foreclosed any hope of understanding between the two countries. Japan's steel industry was small compared to that of the United States. In 1940 the total production of ingot steel in Japan and Korea was about 7.5 million tons; in the same year, American production was about ten times greater. It became doubtful whether there would be enough raw materials to keep this small industry in full production. Therefore, the American iron and steel embargo, plus the restraints which were imposed later on exports of iron ore to Japan, severely hurt her and threatened the entire Japanese economic structure. It forced the Japanese steel industry to operate during the next critical year well below capacity, and it prevented any program of expansion.

Under these circumstances, Japan was compelled to adopt a new policy. She began to expand to the south in order to control those areas which would supply not only the necessities of life, but also the products essential to the Japanese war effort—notably oil, rubber, tin, and adequate foodstuffs.

On July 25, 1941, Roosevelt issued from Hyde Park an executive order, effective the next day, freezing all Japanese assets in the United States. This order brought under government control all financial and import-and-export trade transactions in which Japanese interests were involved. In effect, it created an economic blockade of Japan. Our highest military and naval authorities—among them Admiral Harold

R. Stark, Chief of Naval Operations and General George C. Marshall, Army Chief of Staff—believed that the freezing order would cause Japan to take last-ditch counter measures. Six days before the order was issued, the War Plans Division warned that an embargo on Japan would possibly involve the United States in early war in the Pacific. Dr. Stanley K. Hornbeck, Adviser on Political Relations to the State Department, and Secretaries Morgenthau and Stimson strongly advocated the order.

When the Japanese Ambassador, Admiral Kichisaburo Nomura, called at the Department of State to inquire as to the meaning of the executive order, he was coolly received by Undersecretary of State Sumner Welles. This attitude was discouraging to Nomura, who felt that Japanese-American relations had reached an impasse which held dangerous implications. In Tokyo, Japanese officials held a series of urgent conferences to review the situation and to prepare for war if it should come. "We are convinced," these officials said, "that we have reached the most important, and at the same time, the most critical moment in Japanese-U. S. relations."

The picture was not encouraging. The powerful Japanese Planning Board, which co-ordinated the complex structure of Japan's war economy, found the country's resources meager and only enough, in view of the blockade, for a quick and decisive war. "If the present condition is left unchecked," asserted Teuchi Suzuke, President of the Board, "Japan will find herself totally exhausted and unable to rise in the future." The blockade, he believed, would bring about Japan's collapse within two years, and he urged that a final decision on war or peace be made "without hesitation."

Tojo, then Minister of War, regarded the "freezing order" by the United States as driving Japan "into a tight corner." Oil was vital to Japan, and from now on each fall of the level on oil brought the hour of decision closer. Marquis Kido, the Lord Keeper of the Privy Seal, came to the conclusion that "Japan's lack of oil was so critical that there would be an acute national crisis if there is a mistake in diplomacy." In case of war, he said, "we would have enough only for one and a half years," and a conflict "would be a hopeless one." Fleet Admiral Nagano, supreme naval adviser to the Emperor, declared:

I think one of the large causes of this war was the question of oil. . . . Not only the two services but the civilian elements were extremely interested, because after the U. S., Great Britain and the Netherlands refused to sell any more oil, our country was seriously threatened by the oil shortage; consequently, every element in Japan was keenly interested in the southern regions.

Historian Louis Morton, Chief of the Pacific Section, Department of the Army, wrote that America, by adopting a program of unrestricted economic warfare, left Japan the embarrassing choice of humiliating surrender or resistance by whatever means lay at hand. He termed the American order of July 26 "the Japanese Pearl Harbor," suggesting a degree of provocation in excess of what many have been willing to concede. To Japanese officials it seemed obvious that this constant economic pressure by the Roosevelt Administration was a design to provoke war. . . .

. . . As Japanese military intentions were being projected southward, President Roosevelt and Prime Minister Churchill met at Newfoundland from August 9 to 13, 1941. The Atlantic Conference provided Churchill with sufficiently strong assurances of United States military support in the Far East to enable him to base important wartime military decisions on those assurances. These facts and the complete understandings with which the two leaders parted are attested by Churchill's speech

in the House of Commons as set forth in the *Private Papers of Senator Vandenberg*. The Senator's reaction to the speech was recorded on January 27, 1942:

Churchill spoke to the British Commons today. *And we learned something of very great importance over here in the U. S. A.* In discussing events leading up to the war in the Far Pacific he said: '. . . the probability since the Atlantic Conference, at which *I discussed these matters with President Roosevelt, that the United States, even if not herself attacked, would come into the war in the Far East* and thus make the final victory assured, seemed to allay some of these anxieties, and that expectation has not been falsified by the events.'

In other words, Churchill said that when he met Roosevelt the first time—and wrote 'The Atlantic Charter'—he talked with the President about the fact that Britain must not fight alone in the Far East, and got some sort of an assurance . . . that the U. S. would go to war with Japan *regardless of whether* Japan attacked us or not. In still other words, *we were slated for this war by the President before Pearl Harbor*. Pearl Harbor merely precipitated what was 'in the cards.' To whatever extent this is true, it indicates how both Congress and the Country were in total ignorance of the American war-commitments made by the President and never disclosed.

What stronger evidence can there be that President Roosevelt did make positive commitments of support to Churchill?

In August, 1941, Prime Minister Fumimaro Konoye, realizing the situation with the United States was getting worse, made a proposal to meet with President Roosevelt at Honolulu. Ambassador Joseph C. Grew was so deeply impressed with the sincerity of Konoye's plea that he immediately sent a dispatch to Secretary Hull and urged, "with all the force at his command, for the sake of avoiding the obviously growing possibility of an utterly futile war between Japan and the United States, that this Japanese proposal not be turned aside without very prayerful consideration. . . .

The opportunity is here presented . . . for an act of the highest statesmanship . . . with the possible overcoming thereby of apparently insurmountable obstacles to peace hereafter in the Pacific."

There was "little doubt" that Konoye "would appeal for American cooperation," Grew's communication continued, "in bringing the China affair to a close and would probably be prepared to give far-reaching undertakings in that connection, involving also the eventual withdrawal of Japanese forces from Indochina." The "time element" was "important because the rapid acceleration given by recent American economic measures to the deterioration of Japan's economic life will tend progressively to weaken rather than to strengthen the moderate elements in the country and the hand of the present Cabinet and to reinforce the extremists." In Grew's opinion the "most important aspect of the proposed meeting" was that if the results were "not wholly favorable," there would, nonetheless, be "a definite opportunity to prevent the situation in the Far East from getting rapidly worse."

On August 26, Ambassador Nomura received an urgent message which expressed an almost frantic desire to arrange a meeting between the leaders of the two countries. The instruction stated: "Now the international situation as well as our internal situation is strained in the extreme and we have reached the point where we will pin our last hopes on an interview between the Premier and the President." Two days later the Japanese Ambassador handed President Roosevelt Konoye's proposal for a meeting to "take place as soon as possible." It was rejected.

Since the end of 1940 our Ambassador in Tokyo had pressed for a "thorough reexamination of our approach to the problems of the Far East and a redefinition of the main immediate objectives to be pursued by American diplomacy." Both he and the entire embassy staff were convinced the problem "could never be solved by formulas drawn up in the exploratory conversations." They believed the problem "could and would be solved if the proposed meeting between Prince Konoye and the President should take place." When Ambassador Grew urged President Roosevelt to make a speech at the earliest possible moment in order that the Japanese public would gain knowledge of our true intentions, his "recommendation was not carried out." "Why?" Grew asked: "History will wish to know." In his opinion this gesture "might well have turned the whole trend in Japan at this critical time."

Following the outbreak of war, Grew asked Hull why Konoye's important proposal had not been accepted. Hull answered: "If you thought so strongly, why didn't you board a plane and come to tell us?" The Ambassador reminded him of the urgent telegrams he had repeatedly sent the Department. Suddenly, he "wondered whether Mr. Hull had been given and had read all of the dispatches from Tokyo." There is "no evidence" in the official correspondence, of either a "desire or of efforts on the part of our Government to simplify Prince Konoye's difficult task or to meet him even part way." Ambassador Grew assured the President that Konoye was willing to "go as far as is possible, without incurring open rebellion in Japan, to reach a reasonable understanding with us." He pleaded his case with courage and determination:

It seems to me highly unlikely that this chance will come again or that any Japanese statesman other than Prince Konoye could succeed in controlling the military extremists in carrying through a policy which they, in their ignorance of international affairs and economic laws, resent and oppose. The alternative to reaching a settlement now would be the greatly increased probability of war—*Facillis descensus Averno est*—and while we would undoubtedly win in the end, I question whether it is in our own interest to see an impoverished Japan reduced to the position of a third-rate Power.

A memorandum was prepared in the Far Eastern Division of the Department of State, which attempted to evaluate the arguments, pro and con, regarding the proposed Roosevelt-Konoye meeting. Joseph Ballantine arrived at the conclusion that the arguments against the meeting outweighed those in favor of it. It was feared that if we entered into negotiations with Japan, Chinese morale might be "seriously impaired." In this event "it would probably be most difficult to revive in China the psychology necessary to continue effective resistance against Japan." Lauchlin Currie, Administrative Assistant to the President, strongly emphasized this viewpoint. He was opposed to an American agreement with Japan because it "would do irreparable damage to the good will we have built up in China." Moreover, it was pointed out that the British, Dutch and other governments would entertain "misgivings" about America's will to resist. This could result in a "breakdown in their efforts to maintain a firm front against Japan." Ballantine expressed the view that "such a meeting would create illusions for the Japanese people and would operate as a factor to hide from the Japanese people the wide discrepancy between the viewpoints of the American and the Japanese Governments."

Ambassador Grew seemed to be of the opinion such a meeting would, on the contrary, dispel such illusions. What he thought necessary "was a dramatic gesture, something that would electrify the people both in Japan and the United States and would give impetus to an entirely new trend of thought and policy." Finally, the Ballantine memorandum stated: "The effect of such a meeting upon the American public would in all probability be unfavorable, particularly among those groups which have exhibited an uncompromising stand on the question of stopping Japanese aggression."

[On October 2, 1941,] Secretary Hull rejected the idea of a Konoye-Roosevelt meeting and remarked to Ambassador Nomura that, before there could be a meeting between the President and Prince Konoye, there would first have to be an agreement upon basic principles of policy. He knew that such an agreement was not possible. In other circumstances, Hull's reason might have had validity; in the unique circumstances of the Konoye offer, it had none. The meat of the Konoye offer was that the Emperor would act; preliminary negotiations would serve only to make the Emperor's action doubtful.

The British attitude was generally affirmative with regards to the Konoye offer. They presumed it would serve their interest of securing Singapore and maintaining the stabilization of Southeast Asia. Actually, of course, war did result in the loss of Singapore. However, the record indicates that Sir Robert Craigie, British Ambassador in Tokyo, was "firmly of the opinion" that the Roosevelt-Konoye meeting should be held. In his view "it would be a foolish policy if this superb opportunity is permitted to slip by assuming an unduly suspicious attitude." According to Duff Cooper, Ambassador Craigie stated to the Foreign Office shortly before the fall of Konoye Cabinet, "Time now suitable for real peace with Japan. Hope this time American cynicism will not be allowed to interfere with realistic statesmanship."

The hard-pressed Chinese stood to benefit from failure of the conference and from involvement of Japan in war with the United States. China could win only in a peace following the war. Clarence Gauss, then Ambassador to China, believed it was "indeed vital" to "give China all the support we can in her fight against Japanese aggression." In a message which was received in Washington following the outbreak of war, he wrote:

At the same time I believe that it is important that we bear in mind that the defeat of Japanese aggression does not necessarily entail as many Chinese think, our crushing Japan militarily. The complete elimination of Japan as a force in the Far East would not be conducive either to order or prosperity in this area.

Major General Charles A. Willoughby, who was formerly American Intelligence Chief in the Far East, has testified that Prince Konoye "was desperately serious in effecting a last minute understanding with the United States."

Sentiment within the Department of State was generally unfavorable to the proposed Roosevelt-Konoye meeting. The Treasury Department—which was to play an increasingly formative role in the development of American Far Eastern policy— voiced its firm opposition to any agreement with Japan. The President was warned of the hidden perils of "a new Munich." . . .

Although tension was mounting in Tokyo, Japanese officials did not lose hope that an agreement could be made to avert war. Ambassador Nomura was instructed to present a *modus vivendi* to the Secretary of State, but this was rejected when it became certain the Chinese and the British would not agree. However, Hull went ahead and drafted a *modus vivendi* of his own which President Roosevelt regarded as a "fair proposition" but he was "not very hopeful" of its success.

At noon on November 25, Secretaries Stimson and Knox met at the White House together with General Marshall and Admiral Stark. The discussion dealt mainly with the Japanese situation concerning the intercepted message fixing the November 29 deadline [for setting war plans in motion]. The President "brought up the event that we were likely to be attacked perhaps (as soon as) next Monday, for the Japanese are notorious for making an attack without warning." The main question was *"how we should maneuver them into the position of firing the first shot without allowing too much danger* to ourselves. It was a difficult proposition." This took place before Hull sent his ultimatum on November 26.

The next morning Stimson heard from Hull over the telephone that Hull had "about made up his mind" not to go through with his plan for a three months' truce, but, instead, to "kick the whole thing over" and tell the Japanese that he had no proposition at all. The decision for a *modus vivendi* was thus dropped and the President gave his blessing to the shelving of it in his morning interview with Hull on November 26.

The proposed *modus vivendi* provided for a truce of three months during which time the United States and Japan would agree not to "advance by force or threat of force" in Southeastern and Northeastern Asia or in the southern and northern Pacific area. The Japanese would agree to withdraw their troops from Indochina and to relax their freezing and export restrictions, permitting the resumption of trade in embargoed articles. The United States would modify its restrictions in the same way. The draft of the proposal declared: "The Government of the United States is earnestly desirous to contribute to the promotion and maintenance of peace in the Pacific area and to afford every opportunity for the continuance of discussions with the Japanese Government directed towards working out a broad-gauge program of peace throughout the Pacific area." There had been "some progress" made in regard to "the general principles which constitute the basis of a peaceful settlement covering the entire Pacific area." This proposal was never submitted to the Japanese Government.

Had a *modus vivendi* with Japan been reached—and it could have been reached with far fewer concessions at the expense of China than were later to be made to Soviet Russia at Yalta—almost certainly the war with Japan would thereby have been averted, particularly in view of the German reverses in Russia in the winter of 1941–1942. A growing conviction existed in Japanese military circles that Germany was in a death struggle in her war with Russia. In his testimony before the Congressional Committee investigating the attack on Pearl Harbor, General Marshall said that if the 90-day truce had been effected, the United States might never have become involved in the war at all; that a delay by the Japanese from December, 1941, into January, 1942, might have resulted in a change of Japanese opinion as to the wisdom of the attack because of the collapse of the German front before Moscow in December, 1941.

Why did Secretary Hull change his mind about a *modus vivendi?* It is difficult to get a precise sequence of events which led to the final decision. However, factors which must have influenced the decision were the strong protest from the Chinese, and Churchill's views which were received during the night of November 25.

Another factor which cannot be dismissed was the pressure exerted by Harry Dexter White [of the Treasury Department]. As soon as word of Secretary Hull's offer of a *modus vivendi* became known, White took precipitate action. A letter signed "Henry Morgenthau, Jr." was dispatched to President Roosevelt on the 24th or 25th of November. Its words told of the dire consequences that would come in the wake of any agreement with Japan. "After

our long association, I need not tell you that this is not written in any doubt of your objectives, but I feel and fear that if the people, our people, and all the oppressed people of the earth, interpret your move as an appeasement of repressive forces, as a move that savors strongly of 'selling out China' for a temporary respite, a terrible blow will have struck against those very objectives." The President was reminded of the "supreme part" he was "to play in world affairs." This role could be played "with complete effectiveness if only [he] retain[ed] the people's confidence in [his] courage and steadfastness in the face of aggression, and in the face of the blandishments of temporary advantages." . . .

Pressure exerted by Communist sympathizers in the Institute of Pacific Relations must also be taken into account when analyzing the reasons for the rejection of a truce with Japan. On November 25, Professor Owen Lattimore of Johns Hopkins University, the United States' special adviser to Chiang Kai-shek, dispatched an anxious cable to Presidential Assistant Lauchlin Currie arguing against any agreement between the United States and Japan on a *modus vivendi.*

On the same day Harry Dexter White sent "an urgent telegram" to Edward C. Carter, Secretary General of the Institute of Pacific Relations, asking him to "come to Washington." When Carter arrived the following morning White assured him that everything was all right and "that every friend of China could be satisfied." On that day Secretary Hull changed his mind and decided to "kick the whole thing over" because Chiang Kai-shek felt that the *modus vivendi* proposal "would make a terrifically bad impression in China."

Hull declared later that he dropped the *modus vivendi* proposal largely because "the Chinese Government violently opposed the idea." He testified: "It developed that the conclusion with Japan of such an arrangement would have been a major blow to Chinese morale." There was a "serious risk of collapse of Chinese morale and resistance, and even of disintegration of China." In light of this fact it "became perfectly evident that the *modus vivendi* aspect would not be feasible." . . .

The question arises here as to whether the Chinese did reject this proposal. The Chinese Ambassador denied his Government was blocking the putting into effect of a temporary arrangement which might afford a cooling-off spell in the Far Eastern situation.

There may be grounds for doubt that Lattimore correctly reported Chiang Kai-shek's position. But it is hardly conceivable that he presented the *modus vivendi* to the Generalissimo in a manner designed to gain his acceptance.

Lauchlin Currie may have been one of the key figures in the rejection of a truce with the Japanese. He is reported as having been agitated over the *modus vivendi* until Secretary Hull finally decided to abandon the idea. On November 28, when Currie lunched with Edward C. Carter, he was no longer worried. In place of the *modus vivendi*, Hull had, on November 26, submitted to the Japanese Ambassador ten conditions which Japan found too stiff a price for peace and war was now a foregone conclusion.

"I should think," Carter noted on November 29, "that Currie probably had a terribly anxious time for the past week. For a few days it looked as though Hull was in danger of selling China and America and Britain down the river." But now everything was all right. What Ambassador Grew had called "an utterly futile war" with Japan was now directly ahead.

On the afternoon of November 26, 1941, Secretary Hull abandoned all thought of a truce with Japan and put in final shape the ten-point ultimatum to Japan. The Japanese Ambassadors were given an ultimatum reading: "The Government of Japan will withdraw all military, naval, air and police forces from China and from Indochina." Both Ambassadors were aghast at the "sudden change of attitude."

Admiral Stark and General Marshall had reviewed the Far Eastern situation. They had recommended that "no ultimatum be delivered to Japan." But Hull went ahead with it. Then he told Secretary of War Stimson: "I have washed my hands of it and it is now in the hands of you and Knox—the Army and the Navy."

It is significant that the ultimatum presented by Hull to the Japanese was based upon an explosive memorandum written by Harry Dexter White, a Soviet agent. . . .

On November 18, 1941, Secretary Morgenthau sent to Secretary Hull a long memorandum, drafted by White, with reference to the terms for peace that should be presented to Japan. These terms were so stiff that White knew that Japan could not accept them. He was apparently anxious for war between Japan and the United States because such a conflict would relieve Japanese pressure upon Russia's Far Eastern flank. Russia had over 200,000 men facing Japan in the Far East. These troops were desperately needed in the war against Germany.

On November 19, Maxwell Hamilton, Chief of the Far Eastern Division of the Department of State, revised the White memorandum slightly. He found the memorandum "the most constructive one which I have yet seen." Secretary Hull had both the White memorandum and the Maxwell revision before him when he drafted the ultimatum of November 26. It is significant that in this ultimatum eight of the drastic demands of the White memorandum found a place. In other words, Harry Dexter White, a Soviet agent, helped in an important way to draft the ultimatum that provoked war between Japan and the United States. This was a primary Soviet aim in the Far East. . . .

Neither Roosevelt nor Hull believed that the Japanese would accept the terms embodied in the American note of November 26. Why, then, did they proffer it? Could it be that they meant to provoke Japan to attack the United States so that the latter might get into war with Germany by the "back door"? This is the thesis followed by a number of reputable historians today.

In general, the literature on Japanese-American relations before the war is highly partisan, either charging the Roosevelt Administration with "sinister design" and "warlike intent" or celebrating it as prescient and realistic. PAUL SCHROEDER (b. 1927), a professor of history at the University of Illinois, takes a middle ground between these extremes. Though finding no evidence of a conscious attempt to involve the United States in the war, Schroeder sees other reasons to be critical of Administration policy, picturing Roosevelt and Hull as seeking peace through a popular but inflexible diplomacy which inadvertently pushed Japan into an attack on the United States.*

Paul Schroeder

American Policy Unintentionally Provocative

The Japanese-American negotiations [in 1941] and the policy pursued therein by the United States have been investigated and interpreted a number of times. It is neither possible nor necessary to review those interpretations here. Only three major points in this study are to be injected into the controversy. The first of these has already been made, namely, that the Tripartite Pact was initially a major issue in dispute but soon declined in importance and was used only for propaganda purposes at the end. The other two points are more general. The first is that there was a real change in the positions and the policies of both Japan and the United States in the course of the negotiations, a change which was ultimately of decisive signifi-

cance. The second point is that this change, particularly in American policy, was a development so natural as to appear inevitable and so popular as to be virtually irreversible.

The first of the two points still to be discussed is controversial. The prevailing interpretation of the Japanese-American negotiations is that no change of any importance occurred throughout the talks. In its original and most extreme form, this argument stems from the State Department. Hull and his associates have always maintained flatly that there was no change in the respective positions of the two powers throughout the negotiations. The United States never altered her fundamental policy, which was one of insisting upon

*Reprinted from Paul Schroeder: *The Axis Alliance and Japanese-American Relations, 1941.* Copyright © 1958 by the American Historical Association. Used by permission of the Cornell University Press. Pp. 168–182, 200–203. Footnotes omitted.

Hull's Four Points, the sanctity of treaties, and the principle of being a good neighbor in international relations. "The principles set forth in our November 26 proposal," insisted Hull, "were in all important respects essentially the same principles we had been proposing to the Japanese right along." Japan, on the other hand (so the argument runs), was from first to last bent on a ruthless policy of military expansion. Her sole purpose in the negotiations was to persuade or compel the United States to yield to Japan control of the entire Pacific, from Hawaii to India and beyond. There was nothing the United States could have done which would have deterred Japan from her course of aggression. "It was not within the power of this Government otherwise than by abject submission to Japan's terms, to halt Japan in her course," claimed Hull. "Japan [in August 1941] . . . was on a steady and fixed course of conquest which would reach us in Japan's own chosen time." Her aggression, moreover, was totally senseless and irrational, for the United States was offering Japan everything a peaceful nation could desire. "There was nothing in there [the Ten Points Plan of November 26]," maintained the Secretary, "that any peaceful nation pursuing a peaceful course would not have been delighted to accept." Japan's incurable militarism, however, rendered of no avail all American generosity and patience. The negotiations did nothing more than to reveal the irreconcilable character of the positions of the two governments.

The clash between Japan and the United States, the argument continues, was molded by decades of history. Japan had become inherently belligerent; the United States was inherently peace-loving. The policies of peace which Hull espoused embodied, as he saw it, the practices of historic Americanism. "We have," he as-

serted, "from over an indefinite period in the past stood for all of the doctrines that you see set out [in the Ten Points Plan]." They were, in fact, universal principles, subscribed to by all peaceful men the world over. Nothing in American history resembled Japan's actions in the Pacific. In her own sphere, the Western Hemisphere, the United States had always acted solely in self-defense. The Monroe Doctrine, "as we interpret and apply it uniformly since 1823," said Hull, presumably including thereby also the Roosevelt Corollary, "only contemplates steps for our physical safety." The Japanese New Order, in contrast, was a mere cover-up for aggression. In the same manner, self-defense, equal opportunity, and peace had always been the keynotes of American foreign policy in the Far East. Hull's political adviser, Stanley K. Hornbeck, who yields to no one in defense of historic American Far Eastern policy, writes:

Our people and our Government have, from the very beginning of our national life, asserted that in the commercial relations of sovereign states there should *not* be a "closed door" *anywhere.*

Again:

The intentions of the United States in regard to the Western Pacific and Eastern Asia have always been peaceful intentions. Our procedures have been procedures of peace.

The American acquisitions of Hawaii, Guam, and even of the Philippines, Mr. Hornbeck is careful to point out, are also in reality clear evidences of a peaceful, liberal attitude.

In contrast stood the record of Japanese aggression in the past. Japan had always intended to go to war with the United States. The negotiations in 1941 were merely a sham; Kurusu's mission was simply one of stalling the United States along until Japan was ready to attack, while Nomura served as a blind. The efforts of the so-called "peace party" in Tokyo also were meaningless, the argument runs. For since 1937, according to Hull, Tojo at the head of the military was in "supreme control" of everything Japan possessed, including her Navy and the Emperor. The course of Japanese aggression, moreover, had been determined long before the outbreak at the Marco Polo bridge. Following the advent of the Tanaka cabinet in 1927, Hull maintained, "Japan had consistently been pursuing only one fixed policy—that of expansion by aggression." Part and parcel of this policy was an eventual attack upon the United States. Modern Japan had trained herself well in the execution of such a policy. Her whole history from 1895 to the present was one of international duplicity and military aggrandizement. The Sino-Japanese War of 1894–1895, the Russo-Japanese War of 1904–1905, the Twenty-One Demands of 1915, the Anti-Comintern Pact of 1936—these and many other events formed the pattern sinister.

It is not to be supposed that this extravagant theory still finds many defenders. Most of it is plainly the product of wartime passions and postwar politics. One is tempted to remark, paraphrasing George Bernard Shaw, that even in Washington it is possible to say very foolish things about one's enemies simply because one is at war with them. The underlying idea that no change was possible throughout the negotiations because of Japan's intransigence, however, remains current. [The historian] Basil Rauch, for example, has this to say of the fixed Japanese intent:

Japan in the spring and summer of 1941 would accept no diplomatic arrangement which did not give it everything that it might win in the Far East by aggression, without the trouble and expense of military campaigns.

The careful scholar Herbert Feis, who does not by any means accept the State Department's thesis uncritically, nevertheless contends that the gap between Japan and the United States never really lessened and that neither side fundamentally altered its original stand. The only two changes in their positions, Mr. Feis says, were, first, the Japanese offer to renounce further southwestern advances and to accept less than full victory in China and, second, the attempt by both governments toward the end to seek a *modus vivendi*.

Other authorities could be cited with the same general intent, namely, that there was never any serious prospect of Japanese-American agreement, that the two nations' positions were fundamentally irreconcilable, and that both of them were too committed to opposite goals to change. One hesitates to disagree in the face of their more or less unanimous testimony. Yet it would seem that the basic question is not whether Japan and the United States ever approached agreement or whether they were always at odds. It is true that they never came close to a real settlement. The more important question, however, is whether Japan and the United States were at odds over the same things throughout the conversations—whether the issues that separated them were the same at the end as at the beginning.

Here, it is contended, a real change took place. That some shifts in diplomatic position occurred during the negotiations no one will seriously deny. One needs only to compare the Japanese proposal of May 12 with those of November 7 and 20 and the American plan of May 16 with that of November 26 to see that there was unquestionably a change. Japan was clearly asking for less, and the United States was demanding more, in November than in May. It is also plain that there was a decisive change in regard to one of the major issues in dispute, the Tripartite Pact. These, it is here claimed, were only parts of a greater development. In the summer of 1941, the basic aims of both Japanese and American foreign policy underwent an important transformation. The result was that their basic quarrel in November was no longer the same as it had been in May.

Until approximately the middle of July 1941 the policy of Japan was unmistakably aggressive in nature. Her goals were expansionistic, although she was becoming more and more apprehensive and doubtful about attaining them. She was still committed to ending the China conflict on her own terms. She still hoped to have her puppet government headed by Wang Ching-wei coalesced into the Chinese government, with Japan preserving a very large measure of military and economic control within China. Furthermore, she had definite plans for southward expansion as far as possible—certainly into French Indo-China and Thailand and if circumstances allowed also into the Netherlands East Indies. The diplomatic methods she used to implement her program showed similarly a policy of offense. Her browbeating of the Vichy French and high-pressure negotiation with the Dutch over the East Indies testify to this. She still expected a German victory, counting on it and the Tripartite Pact to isolate the United States and persuade America not to interfere in the Pacific. The last, rather desperate expressions of this policy of offense are the resolutions of the Imperial Conference of July 2. Here Japan resolved, in spite of the danger of war with the United States and Great Britain, to press on with her previously prepared plans for expansion southward. The final overt act in the Japanese campaign was the occupation of southern Indo-China in late July, a move already determined over a month before as part of the old expansionist policy.

The American position in the Far East in this same period was definitely defensive. As has been shown, the United States policy was one of holding the line in Asia, while building up her home defenses and concentrating on aid to Great Britain in Europe. The United States had thus two essential and immediate objectives in Asia: first, stopping Japan from any further advance southward that would menace the British supply line and, second, keeping Japan out of the European war. To help accomplish these objectives, a major aim of American diplomacy was to persuade Japan to withdraw from the Tripartite Pact, even if only by degrees. The remaining American goal, the liberation of China, was of necessity a distinctly subsidiary and remote one. As Ambassador Grew wrote in November 1940:

We need not aim to drive Japan out of China now. That can be taken care of, perhaps, if and after Britain wins the war with Germany. But stopping Japan's proposed far-flung southward advance and driving her out of China are two different matters. We can tolerate her occupation of China for the time being, just as we have tolerated it for the past three years. I doubt if we should tolerate any great extension of the southward advance.

Throughout the first half of 1941 the American position was plainly that, although she would aid China within limits to keep Japan occupied there, she did not intend to go to war for the sake of China. She would, however, go to war to defend American territory and probably also that of the British and the Dutch in Asia. Even the crucial freezing orders, strong measures though they were, were entirely consistent with the defensive nature of the American policy. They were imposed because the Japanese, having moved into southern Indo-China, were in a position gravely menacing all of southeastern Asia. The freezing orders were to teach Japan that she had gone far enough—indeed, too far—and that she must now begin to retreat.

The embargo produced precisely the result intended. Japan, faced with the consequences of her move, began to recoil. The struggle within Japan for the control of policy took a decided turn for the better (from the American point of view), with the initiative passing into the hands of moderates such as Konoye and Toyoda. The brave promises and boastful programs of Japanese expansionism, like those of the resolutions of July 2, were for the moment ignored or forgotten, as Japan went clearly on the defensive. Her main objective now was somehow to extricate herself from the desperate position in which she was entangled, to get relief from the inexorable economic pressure of the embargo, and to avoid what seemed to be inevitable war. She was not concerned for the time with expanding her empire; the problem was now one of salvaging as much as she could. To gain peace or at least a breathing spell, she was willing to make what seemed to her to be two major concessions. She was ready to take a course independent of Germany and indifferent to the Tripartite Pact. She was also willing to stop her southward advance and even, at the end, to withdraw from her latest acquisition, southern Indo-China. The one thing she would not do was to evacuate China and to renounce her aims there. This in her eyes was impossible. She could modify her terms somewhat, but the retention of a considerable economic and military hold, particularly on North China, was considered by her military leaders absolutely indispensable, for political reasons if for none other. There are a number of moves in this period which indicate the defensive character of Japanese policy—the rift with Germany, Konoye's invitation to Roosevelt to attend the Leaders' Conference, the postponement of the decision for war even after the fall of Konoye, and the last-min-

ute proposals of November 20. The fall of Konoye and the accession of Tojo did not really change Japanese policy but merely presaged its ultimate failure. The real difference between Konoye and Tojo was not that the one wanted peace and the other war. It was rather that, when each was faced with a choice between war and humiliating terms, Konoye would waver indefinitely, while Tojo would choose war.

The policy of the United States, meanwhile, underwent a corresponding change: America went on the diplomatic offensive after July 1941. Her aims were no longer simply those of holding the line against Japanese advances and of inducing Japan to draw away from an alliance which the United States considered menacing. The chief objective of American policy now was to push Japan back, to compel her to withdraw from her conquests. The United States was determined to see that Japan assumed such a peaceful attitude in Asia that she could never again threaten the security of her neighbors. She was to renounce her dream of hegemony in Asia, to give up her plans for expansion, and to accept defeat in China. The objective that had previously been the least important and pressing in American policy, the liberation of China, now became the crucial consideration. American diplomats made a prompt and total evacuation of Japanese troops the *sine qua non* for agreement. The weapon of severe economic pressure on Japan, which had been forged and used by the United States, up to and including the time of the freezing orders, to hold the line against Japanese expansion, now was employed to enforce the American demands for the evacuation of China. The Japanese were given to understand that there would be no relaxation of the embargo until Japan gave up her gains by aggression there.

The old defensive goals were not forgotten. They remained uppermost especially in the minds of American military planners. The military strategists continued to insist to the end that the primary objectives of American policy should remain the defeat of Germany and the exclusion of Japan from the war. Brigadier General Leonard T. Gerow, acting Assistant Chief of Staff, maintained that even the impending defeat of China would not warrant involvement of the United States in a war with Japan. Chief of Staff General George Marshall and Admiral Harold R. Stark agreed with Gerow. The reports prepared by the Army Intelligence Service from July to December 1941 all display a single consistent point of view, along with a number of important insights. First was the belief that the European war remained uppermost and that the previous essentially defensive objectives pursued by the United States in the Far East should be maintained. Second was a recognition of the estrangement between Japan and Germany and of the completely altered Japanese attitude toward the Tripartite Pact. Third was a belief that the Konoye government was really trying to extricate Japan from her difficulties without war. Brigadier General Miles, in charge of Army Intelligence, believed that the United States might gain her essential objectives through the use of "strong diplomacy," provided that she made sure that Konoye could carry the Japanese Army and Navy with him in his policy. Fourth and most important was the conviction that it was unnecessary, and probably even harmful, for the United States to insist on an immediate evacuation of China.

This last point, of course, touches the very heart of the whole Japanese-American controversy. The argument of the Army Intelligence Service with regard to it is important enough to be given close attention. Colonel Hayes A. Kroner, acting Assistant Chief of Staff of the Service, supplies this in a memorandum of October

2. The first reason why the United States should not insist on the evacuation of China was that such a move would be impossible for Japan for political reasons:

This division is of the belief that the present Cabinet in Tokyo [Konoye's third cabinet] does not yet feel strong enough to enforce any order for withdrawal of Japanese troops from China, even though under pressure from the United States, it might be inclined to do so.

The move, Kroner maintained, would thus be disastrous for the Konoye regime. Worse, it also "would be highly detrimental to our interests." The removal of so many troops from China back to the Japanese homeland would create grave internal problems for Japan. The civilian government might well be unable to prevent a military explosion leading directly to war with the United States. In addition, with Japanese troops freed from China the threat to Siberia and the southwest Pacific would be gravely increased. "In other words," Kroner concluded, "we must cease at once our attempts to bring about the withdrawal of Japanese armed forces from China."

Ironically enough, at the same time that Kroner was issuing this warning the very events which he feared were taking place. On this same day, October 2, Hull delivered to the Japanese an Oral Statement rejecting the Konoye proposals. It killed the chances for a Leaders' Conference and made certain the downfall of the Konoye government in Japan. The main reason for the American refusal to deal with Konoye, as already seen, was Japan's unwillingness to evacuate China. Thus, at this very time, the Konoye government was tottering to its fall and carrying its hope for peace in the Pacific with it because it could not budge the American diplomats from their insistence that Japanese troops had to get out of China forthwith. And all the while, American military planners were urging that the United States ought by all means to let the Japanese stay. The clash between the United States strategic interests and her diplomatic policy cannot be seen more plainly.

Other men outside the military remembered the old defensive goals. Ambassador Grew, as shown, repeatedly urged that the President should make an attempt to meet Konoye halfway. His main argument was that the strong American action in the embargo had created the opportunity for the United States to gain her essential aims, if only she did not insist on getting everything at once. "History will determine," he wrote later, "whether this opportunity was missed by an attempt to achieve at once our long-range objectives, an utter impossibility under the circumstances then obtaining, at the expense of the immediately vital and essential interests of our country." As for the President, his actions up to the very eve of Pearl Harbor indicate that his interest was primarily centered on Europe. He was particularly concerned with the Far East only as it affected the European war, and the China question for him was secondary.

What happened, then, was not that the original defensive goals were forgotten, but that they were submerged. As Japan began to retreat and as the United States grew steadily stronger, the original problems lost their former urgency. Once the rift between Germany and Japan became plain and the American naval activities in the Atlantic went unnoticed by Japan, there was no longer any real need to worry about the Tripartite Pact. Objectionable it might still be, but hardly dangerous. Moreover, the failure of the Japanese, after the occupation of south Indo-China, to carry farther the program of southward expansion as determined on July 2 diminished at least for the moment the imminent danger of a move to the south. At the same time, Japan's repeated pledges not to

extend her advance any farther south and to withdraw from Indo-China upon reaching peace with China, backed up at the end by an offer of immediate evacuation of south Indo-China, indicated that the southward drive was not an immutable part of Japanese policy. Any concessions the Japanese made, however, did them no good. In the wave of reaction against Japan's move into south Indo-China, the initiative in American policy had passed into the hands of those leaders who had long advocated a strong, no-compromise, no-appeasement stand against Japan. These men—Morgenthau, Knox, Stimson, and others—backed up Hull in his uncompromising principles in order to carry through a modern policy of "thorough." Japan was not merely to be contained and held back, but to be squeezed and harried until she conformed, that is, until she disgorged her gains and abandoned her evil ways.

In one way, the policy thus conceived and executed was indeed a development of historic American policy in the Far East. The United States had long upheld, at least on paper, the cause of China's integrity and independence. For an equally long period she had, for reasons of democratic idealism and commercial self-interest, stood for the Open Door in China. The lively interest felt by Americans over the fate of China was always an important factor in Japanese-American relations and could easily grow, as it did, into the paramount consideration. But in another sense the change in policy was a reversal of a historic American position. For it was also a long-standing American policy, equally as traditional as the Open Door and far more consistently observed in practice, that the United States would not go to war for the sake of China. This policy was now in effect overthrown. American diplomats made it clear that the United States would accept war with Japan in preference to any settlement between Japan and China which did not restore intact China's territorial and administrative integrity. It is commonly agreed that this was the one real cause of the war. Had the China issue been solved or left to one side, the other two problems could surely have been adjusted without open conflict. In insisting that the Japanese withdraw immediately and completely from China and in employing the weapon of extreme economic pressure to compel Japanese agreement, the United States was carrying out a new offensive policy which made the crucial difference between peace and war.

It would be entirely wrong to suppose that this change in policy was simply the reasoned decision of policy makers. It would be still worse to charge that it represents the underhanded maneuverings of an administration leading the nation by a back road into war. The shift in policy, decisive though it was in its effects, was a very natural development. In a sense, it was truly and tragically inevitable. For years the United States had been exerting a gradually growing pressure on Japan in an effort to hold her at bay, a pressure conceived as a countermeasure to the outward thrust of Japanese expansion and reaching its climax in the joint freezing orders. American foreign policy would have had to be extraordinarily sensitive to the changed situation and unusually flexible to have prevented the United States from going on the offensive too strongly. The moment that Japan began to draw back, the very force being exerted against her, unless relaxed, would automatically carry the United States to the offense. The measures designed to restrain Japan would serve equally well to force her back.

Moreover, even had the administration wanted to relax the pressure on Japan, this would have been very difficult to do. Chief among the reasons was public opinion. Over the course of a decade, the American

people had built up a profound hatred and distrust of Japan. When the time came that the United States could put heavy pressure on the Japanese, it was the moment the public had long awaited. Virtually no one wanted the pressure relaxed. The most influential writers, politicians, and newspapers called for even more, and when at the very end there arose some concern over the probable consequences of this uncompromising policy, it was already too late. . . .

In judging American policy toward Japan in 1941, it might be well to separate what is still controversial from what is not. There is no longer any real doubt that the war came about over China. Even an administration stalwart like Henry L. Stimson and a sympathetic critic like Herbert Feis concur in this. Nor is it necessary to speculate any longer as to what could have induced Japan to launch such an incredible attack upon the United States and Great Britain as occurred at Pearl Harbor and in the south Pacific. One need not, as Winston Churchill did in wartime, characterize it as "an irrational act" incompatible "with prudence or even with sanity." The Japanese were realistic about their position throughout; they did not suddenly go insane. The attack was an act of desperation, not madness. Japan fought only when she had her back to the wall as a result of America's diplomatic and economic offensive.

The main point still at issue is whether the United States was wise in maintaining a "hard" program of diplomatic and economic pressure on Japan from July 1941 on. Along with this issue go two subsidiary questions: the first, whether it was wise to make the liberation of China the central aim of American policy and the immediate evacuation of Japanese troops a requirement for agreement; the second, whether it was wise to decline Premier Konoye's invitation to a meeting of leaders in the Pacific. On all these points, the policy which the United States carried out still has distinguished defenders. The paramount issue between Japan and the United States, they contend, always was the China problem. In her China policy, Japan showed that she was determined to secure domination over a large area of East Asia by force. Apart from the legitimate American commercial interests which would be ruined or excluded by this Japanese action, the United States, for reasons of her own security and of world peace, had sufficient stake in Far Eastern questions to oppose such aggression. Finally, after ten years of Japanese expansion, it was only sensible and prudent for the United States to demand that it come to an end and that Japan retreat. In order to meet the Japanese threat, the United States had a perfect right to use the economic power she possessed in order to compel the Japanese to evacuate their conquered territory. If Japan chose to make this a cause for war, the United States could not be held responsible.

A similar defense is offered on the decision to turn down Konoye's Leaders' Conference. Historians may concede, as do Langer and Gleason, that Konoye was probably sincere in wanting peace and that he "envisaged making additional concessions to Washington, including concessions on the crucial issue of the withdrawal of Japanese troops from China." But, they point out, Konoye could never have carried the Army with him on any such concession. If the United States was right in requiring Japan to abandon the Co-Prosperity Sphere, then her leaders were equally right in declining to meet with a Japanese Premier who, however conciliatory he might have been personally, was bound by his own promises and the exigencies of Japanese politics to maintain this national aim. In addition, there was the serious possibility that much could be lost from such a meeting—the confidence of China, the cohesiveness of the coalition with Great Britain and Russia. In short, there was not enough prospect of gain to merit taking the chance.

This is a point of view which must be taken seriously. Any judgment on the wisdom or folly of the American policy, in fact, must be made with caution—there are no grounds for dogmatic certainty. The opinion here to be developed, nonetheless, is that the American policy from the end of July to December was a grave mistake. It should not be necessary to add that this does not make it treason. There is a "back door to war" theory, espoused in various forms by Charles A. Beard, George Morgenstern, Charles C. Tansill, and, most recently, Rear Admiral Robert A. Theobald, which holds that the President chose the Far East as a rear entrance to the war in Europe and to that end deliberately goaded the Japanese into an attack. This theory is quite different and quite incredible. It is as impossible to accept as the idea that Japan attacked the United States in a spirit of overconfidence or that Hitler pushed the Japanese into war. Roosevelt's fault, if any, was not that of deliberately provoking the Japanese to attack, but of allowing Hull and others to talk him out of impulses and ideas which, had he pursued them, might have averted the conflict. Moreover, the mistake (assuming that it was a mistake) of a too hard and rigid policy with Japan was, as has been pointed out, a mistake shared by the whole nation, with causes that were deeply organic. Behind it was not sinister design or warlike intent, but a sincere and uncompromising adherence to moral principles and liberal doctrines.

In addition to their arguments that Roosevelt deceived the public and purposely provoked the Japanese, revisionist writers have consistently taken issue with the official explanation for the surprise assault on Pearl Harbor as primarily the fault of negligent field commanders. In revisionist writings, the responsibility rests with Roosevelt and Washington officials who foresaw and welcomed the attack as a means of taking the United States into the war without debate or dissent. The following selection by GEORGE MORGENSTERN (b. 1906), a newspaper writer and member of the *Chicago Tribune* editorial board, is representative of this viewpoint.*

George Morgenstern

Pearl Harbor:
Washington to Blame

On December 6 [1941] a "pilot message" from Tokyo had been decoded [through "Magic"] informing the Embassy in Washington that, having "deliberated deeply on the American proposal of the twenty-sixth of November," it was transmitting a reply in fourteen parts which was to be kept secret pending receipt of later instructions relative to the time when it should be transmitted to the United States government. This notice was in the hands of Hull, Stimson, and others by 3:00 P.M.

The first thirteen parts were transmitted and were in the hands of Navy Communications Intelligence by 2:51 P.M. They were transmitted that night to Mr. Roosevelt, Secretary [of the Navy] Knox, and various high officers of the Army and Navy. It is a disputed point whether Secre-

tary Hull saw them the night of the sixth. The evidence indicates that he was at least informed of their purport by Secretary Knox. Secretary Stimson professed inability to recall whether they were delivered to him, but Knox twice called him after 8:30 that night. As a result of these conversations, Stimson asked the Navy Department on Saturday evening to furnish him by nine o'clock Sunday morning the following information: Compilation of men-of-war in Far East: British, American, Japanese, Dutch, Russian; *also compilation of American men-of-war in Pacific Fleet, with locations,* with a list of American men-of-war in the Atlantic without locations.

The testimony is clear, however, that the "pilot message" was delivered in the afternoon to everyone of importance. How,

*From George Morgenstern, "The Actual Road to Pearl Harbor," in *Perpetual War for Perpetual Peace* edited by Dr. Harry Elmer Barnes, pp. 370–383. Published by the Caxton Printers, Ltd., Caldwell, Idaho, and quoted by permission. Footnotes omitted.

under the circumstances, knowing that the ensuing message in fourteen parts would mark the *de facto* rupture and breaking of negotiations, any of these officials could have remained indifferent to its contents is a mystery. Especially should this have been true because, in all Japanese wars of modern times, the severance of relations was timed to coincide with the outbreak of hostilities and this, in turn, was inaugurated by a surprise attack on the enemy fleet. This had been true in the war with China in 1895, the attack on Port Arthur opening the war with Russia in 1904, and in the war with Germany launched at Tsingtao in 1914. These facts had been pointed out and should have been familiar to all responsible officials.

Yet, according to statements before the [Pearl Harbor] congressional [investigating] committee, not only did Secretaries Hull and Stimson fail to receive the thirteen parts on the night of the sixth but the operating chiefs of the Army and Navy, General Marshall and Admiral Stark, also did not. Stark, having been apprised that this vital message was coming in, went to dinner and the theater. General Marshall suffered a famous case of amnesia and never was able to recall for certain where he was the night of the sixth. When the thirteen parts were submitted to the Secretary of the General Staff, Colonel (later General) Walter Bedell Smith, he took no steps to bring them to Marshall's immediate attention, although, as the Army Board remarked, war by then "was not a question of fact; it was only a question of time."

What about the President? The thirteen parts were taken to the White House the night of the sixth. Roosevelt was having a dinner party for a British vice admiral. The message was left with the request "to get word to the President that this was very urgent." The naval aide on duty was to interrupt Roosevelt's dinner party and

let him see it as soon as possible. Shortly after 9:30 P.M., Lieutenant L. R. Schulz, assistant naval aide, delivered the intercept to Roosevelt in the President's study. With Roosevelt was Harry Hopkins, who paced back and forth as the President read. Having finished, Roosevelt handed the papers to Hopkins, who also read them. According to Schulz, Roosevelt then turned to Hopkins and said in substance, "This means war."

Hopkins, in reply, said that since war was imminent and that the Japanese intended to strike when they were ready, at a moment that was most opportune for them, and that since war was going to come at their convenience, *"it was too bad that we could not strike the first blow and prevent any sort of surprise."* [1]

The President nodded and then said, *"No, we can't do that.* We are a democracy and a peaceful people." Then he raised his voice. He said, *"But we have a good record."* [1]

Roosevelt, while Schulz was still in the room, asked the White House operator to attempt to reach Admiral Stark. Informed that Stark was at the theater, he said he would reach the Admiral later—that he could get him "within perhaps another half hour in any case"—and that he *"did not want to cause public alarm."*

Familiar themes run through these comments. It was "too bad," but it was undeniably a fact, that "we could not strike the first blow and prevent any sort of surprise." Japan was being given the first blow, and, with it, the opportunity for surprise, for it was necessary (according to orders sent to the field at the President's direct instruction) that Japan "commit the first overt act." As phrased by Stimson, "The question was how we should maneuver them into firing the first shot without allowing too much danger to ourselves."

---

[1] Italics supplied.

So, when it was remarked that it was "too bad" that the United States would not fire the first shot and head off the surprise, the President could only echo, "No, we can't do that." And when he said, "But we have a good record," to whom was he referring? To the American people, who had no record at all, because no voice, in moves toward war, or in the situation that had developed in relation to Japan? Or to himself, his administration, and his close associates, who had made the record and had managed it so cleverly that now they were about to be liberated from the party platform pledge, "We will not participate in foreign wars, and we will not send our Army, naval, or air forces to fight in foreign lands outside of the Americas, *except in case of attack*"?[1]

For the moment of liberation was here: "This means war." The President knew it.

Convinced of that fact, knowing that Japan was soon to get in the first shot, knowing that the blow would fall within the territory and possessions of the United States, knowing that Japan was being allowed the opportunity of surprise, what did Roosevelt do? The attack would not come at Pearl Harbor for almost sixteen hours. Much can be done in sixteen hours. One thing that the President did was to talk on the telephone to Stark upon his return from the theater. Stark professed inability to recall this fact independently. Another naval officer, Captain Krick, who had been in the theater party, jogged his memory. Stark could recall nothing of the conversation, so he said.

Captain Krick said Stark went to his upstairs study and returned after five or ten minutes. Krick was not told, but deduced, that Stark must have talked to the President. All that Stark told him was that "conditions in the Pacific were serious . . .

---

[1] Italics supplied.

that conditions with Japan were in a serious state . . . something of that sort. . . ."

Stark could "only assume," on the basis of having been told by Krick, that when he talked with Roosevelt the President mentioned the thirteen parts, but that *"he did not, certainly did not, impress me that it was anything that required action."* So, accepting Stark's account, the President, having decided that "this means war," did not think that that "was anything that required action." . . .

On the following morning, despite overnight developments, very few people acted as if anything required action. Marshall, still supposedly ignorant of the first thirteen parts of the Japanese final reply, went on a leisurely two-and-one-half-hour horseback ride and did not reach his office until 11:25 A.M., two hours before the impending sunrise attack at Pearl Harbor. Stark was in his office somewhere between 8:30 and 11:30 o'clock. Accounts vary.

Hull, Stimson, and Knox, apparently by appointment of Knox the previous night, gathered at the State Department at 10:00 A.M. In the newspapers that morning was a summary of Knox's annual report as Secretary of the Navy. It said that the American people "may feel fully confident in their Navy," that it was "without superior" and "second to none."

The picture presented by Mr. Roosevelt after breakfast and before lunch, was one of studied ease. He had "dedicated this day to rest. Today, tieless and in shirt sleeves, he hoped to catch up with his neglected stamp collection. The President might have been any one of a million Americans putting in a loafing Sunday with a crony and a hobby. Mr. Roosevelt expected war—but not this week end." The crony was Hopkins.

Meanwhile, much had been happening, but nothing was done about it. At five o'clock that morning the message fixing the time of delivery of the Japanese note was available in the Navy Department. It read: "Will the Ambassador please submit to the United States Government (if possible, to the Secretary of State) our reply to the United States at 1:00 P.M. on the 7th, your time."

Other messages from Tokyo disclosed that the showdown was at hand. "All concerned," said one, "regret very much that due to failure in adjusting Japanese-American relations, matters have come to what they are now. . . ." Another referred to the "unprecedented crisis," suggesting that what was to come was a test unique in the annals of Japan, and praying that Japanese officials in the United States "will continue in good health." Inasmuch as none had complained of poor health, the implication was that they faced an altered condition not of a happy nature. An internment camp was the obvious answer. Still another directed Ambassador Nomura to destroy his sole surviving cipher machine and all machine codes and secret documents—an act invariably associated with the coming of war.

Why, in view of all these messages, and what had gone before, Mr. Roosevelt and everyone around him should not have expected war on this particular week end is not easily explained.

Finally, before 8:00 A.M., Navy Intelligence had ready for responsible members of the government and high command the fourteenth and final part of Japan's memorandum. If it had taken no expert interpretation to determine that the first thirteen parts "meant war," as the President had determined, the concluding section of the message made that unmistakably clear, for it used bellicose language in reference to Anglo-American designs and declared that the hope of Japan "to preserve and promote the peace of the Pacific through co-operation with the American Government has finally been lost." When peace

and the hope of peace are lost, what is left? What, indeed, but war?

The first order of business of subordinate officers in possession of the decoded messages was to seek out the high officers of the government and of the Army and Navy who would be concerned with the momentous decisions arising from these statements. It was the earnest desire of some, at least, of these officers to communicate their ideas of how the messages were to be evaluated, with specific reference to the military deductions that were to be drawn from them.

But the duty of evaluation already reposed with the ten men in Washington— the high officials of the government and the Army and Navy. By official order, delivery of the English texts of the intercepted messages was confined, within the War Department, to the Secretary of War (Stimson), the Chief of Staff (Marshall), the Chief of the War Plans Division (Gerow), and the Chief of the Military Intelligence Division (Miles); within the Navy, to the Secretary of the Navy (Knox), the Chief of Naval Operations (Stark), the Chief of the War Plans Division (Turner), and the Director of Naval Intelligence (Wilkinson); to Mr. Roosevelt in the White House, and to Harry Hopkins.

General Miles testified that this restricted circulation was the result of a policy of "closing in on the secret." The commanders at Oahu were denied the flow of code messages, although Admiral [Husband E.] Kimmel received a few texts irrelevant to his station—enough, only, to constitute "affirmative misrepresentation," for he had asked for all vital information, and these few messages persuaded him that he was getting it.

In relieving the commanders in Hawaii of the opportunity of evaluating "Magic," the high officials in Washington inescapably assumed the responsibility, especially the responsibility of instructing their field commanders in the light of information in their possession alone. What, on the morning of December 7, was the nature of this information, and what the responsibility? To this fundamental question, the Navy Court of Inquiry answered: "In the early forenoon of December 7, the War and Navy Departments had information which appeared to indicate that a break in diplomatic relations was imminent, and, by inference and deduction, that an attack in the Hawaiian area could be expected soon."

That the Court confined its reference to knowledge by the War and Navy Departments was a direct result of limiting orders that it should report "whether any offenses have been committed or serious blame incurred on the part of any person or persons in the Naval service," thereby removing from the sphere of its inquiry the determination of responsibility of civilian officials. Despite the fact that it was hardly likely that any board of officers would have had the temerity to criticize the President, the Secretaries of War and Navy, or the Secretary of State, the Army Pearl Harbor Board, operating under somewhat broader terms of reference than the Navy Court, did just that. Among those responsible for the Pearl Harbor disaster, it listed Secretary Hull.

Officers entrusted with the distribution of the latest intercepts on the morning of December 7 were at no loss in determining that this information was of vital and threatening character, demanding immediate action. Colonel R. S. Bratton, chief of the Far Eastern section, Military Intelligence, stated that when he saw the one o'clock delivery message he dropped everything, as it meant to him that Japan planned to attack the United States at or near one o'clock that day.

Other officers concerned with bringing to the attention of high Washington authorities these crucial decoded Japanese messages in the final hours before action had even shrewder and more specific surmises relative to their meaning. Among them were Captain A. H. McCollum, head of the Far Eastern section of Naval Intelligence, and Captain Alwyn D. Kramer, who occupied the Japanese desk in Naval Intelligence.

Captain McCollum testified that on the morning of December 7, perhaps as early as 8:30 o'clock, he discussed the significance of the fourteenth and final part of the Japanese memorandum with Admiral Stark and with Admiral Wilkinson, chief of Naval Intelligence. While they were talking, the instruction to Nomura directing one o'clock delivery was brought in. Stark "immediately called the White House on the telephone, and the draft was taken over to the Secretary of State and the White House." To this McCollum added, "At the time, the possible significance of the time of delivery was pointed out to all hands."

As McCollum later explained, "all hands" meant Stark, Wilkinson, Admiral Ingersoll, assistant chief of operations under Stark, and Captain Schuirmann, liaison officer with the State Department. But all of these officers had responsibilities to the civil leaders of government, and Stark called Roosevelt.

What was the "possible significance," as pointed out by McCollum to his fellow officers? It was that 1:00 P.M., Washington time, was about 7:30 in the morning, Honolulu time. It was also very early morning at that hour in the Far East, and "if an attack were coming, it looked like the timing was such that it was timed for operations out in the Far East and possibly on Hawaii at the time. ... We felt that there were important things which would move at that time, and that was pointed out not only to Admiral Stark but I know it was pointed out to the Secretary of State."

Captain Kramer, who went over with the completed fourteen-part message and the one o'clock delivery dispatch for delivery to Hull, Stimson, and Knox, had "instructions to point out the time business to the Secretary [Hull]." This was an order. So important were these final dispatches that the Navy undertook to deliver them to the Secretary of State although that was the Army's job. Stark and his subordinates did not want to lose a moment's time.

"Now, the danger wasn't in Washington," pointed out Senator [Homer] Ferguson. "The danger wasn't in Washington, because of which you were delivering this message out of the ordinary rules to the Secretary of State. The danger was on our fronts, was it not, and our outposts?"

McCollum agreed. Suggestion, he said, *"was definitely made that a dispatch be sent to the Fleet pointing out that something could be expected to happen at that time."*

The suggestion was that the dispatch be sent to the fleet. The fleet was at Pearl Harbor. So the interpretation of the one o'clock delivery was that something—obviously, attack—could be expected at the corresponding hour in Pearl Harbor and no place else. Suggestion was not made that a warning be sent anywhere else. Directly after this suggestion, Stark tried to get in touch with Marshall by telephone, but the Chief of Staff was still out cantering.

At or about 10:00 A.M. Captain Kramer arrived at Hull's office, where the Secretary of State was sitting down with Stimson and Knox. Stark had already called Hull. Kramer bore the crucial Japanese messages. It was Kramer who first pointed out the significance of the one o'clock delivery. One o'clock, Washington time, was dark night over East Asia and 2:00 A.M. at Manila, but 7:30 A.M., an hour and four minutes after sunrise, at Hawaii. That

hour was "probably the quietest time of the week aboard ship at Pearl Harbor." A large percentage of the crew would be ashore. The crew would be in the process of being piped in for breakfast. It was a military axiom that the hour around dawn was the most favorable period for surprise air attack. And Sunday, as the quietest time of the week aboard ship, was the most favorable day.

At the State Department Kramer pointed out that one o'clock in Washington meant dawn, or 7:30 A.M., in Hawaii. Spread before Stimson was the information he had requested the previous night from the Navy Department: the compilation of all men-of-war in the Far East, also the compilation of American men-of-war in the Pacific Fleet, with locations. Tying together the one o'clock delivery time factor pointing to Pearl Harbor and the location of the bulk of the Pacific Fleet, also at Pearl Harbor, was an elementary mental exercise—all that was required to show where the danger lay. This computation had been worked out by Captain McCollum.

"Were you surprised when the Japanese attacked on Sunday morning at Hawaii?" asked Senator Ferguson.

"I was not surprised at the Japanese attack, sir," the Captain responded. "I was astonished at the success attained by that attack, sir."

Captain McCollum had "for many years felt that in the event of an outbreak of hostilities between the United States and Japan that the Japanese would attempt to strike the Fleet at or near the commencement time of these hostilities." If the fleet had been at San Pedro, he would have anticipated the attack there. "I felt that the fact that the Japanese intended to go to war carried with it the possibility of an attack on the Fleet wherever it might be, sir." The one o'clock delivery time merely reinforced a deduction long entertained.

So, with all of these intimations of what was afoot, with three hours still in which to get a warning to the fleet commander, what did Hull, Knox, and Stimson discuss or do? By way of action, they did nothing. They discussed, by the showing of Stimson's diary, the progress of the Japanese troop transports into the Gulf of Siam, upon which their minds in these last days had so constantly dwelt—dwelt because here was a conflict between the private determination of Roosevelt and his "War Cabinet" that "we must fight" and the constitutional impediments to executing that decision.

Yet, though Mr. Stimson indicates no consideration of the danger to Pearl Harbor, he was to say, after the attack, "Well, I was not surprised!" The three conferees carried on, by the Secretary of War's showing, a highly irrelevant seminar expressing their doubts and fears concerning what might impend in southeast Asia.

In his diary notations, Stimson said, "Today is the day that the Japanese are going to bring their answer to Hull, and everything in Magic indicated that they had been keeping the time back until now in order to accomplish something hanging in the air. . . . Hull is very certain that the Japs are planning some deviltry and we are all wondering where the blow will strike. We three stayed in conference until lunch time, going over the plans for what should be said or done. The main thing is to hold the main people who are interested in the Far East together—the British, ourselves, the Dutch, the Australians, the Chinese."

Hull gave "the broad picture of it" and Knox "also had his views as to the importance of showing immediately how these different nations must stand together." Stimson had them record their statements.

Hull argued that "the defense must be commenced within the South Sea area at such time and places as in the judgment of naval and military experts would be within sufficient time and at such strategic points as would make it most effective. In no other way can it be satisfactorily determined that the Pacific area can be successfully defended."

This was a brief in support of Presidential declarations of war at the discretion of the Executive and his military advisers. It had no possible reference to the constitutional requirement that only Congress "shall have power . . . to declare war." Further, it takes but slight acquaintance with the decisions of the Singapore staff conference [of American, British and Dutch officers in April, 1941] and with the recommendations of Marshall and Stark on November 5 and 27 to detect that Hull was engaged in special pleading in support of a course of action which would take the Administration off the hook—dangling, as it was, between the commitments it had extended to other Powers and the constitutional limitations upon Executive action.

Knox dictated the familiar view that America's destinies were tied up with the fate of the British and Dutch colonial possessions, postulated that "any threat to any one of the three of us is a threat to all of us," and declared for a warning to the Japanese "that any movement in a direction that threatens the United States will be met by force"—a *non sequitur* of majestic proportions in view of what had gone just before.

Then Knox got himself into accord with Hull on the desirability of giving the President a free hand in deciding when the United States should be at war. "The President," he said, "will want to reserve to himself just how to define this." Then, as "suggestions to shoot at," he repeated the lines of prohibition upon Japanese military movements originally defined at the Singapore conference and repeated twice in November by the Chief of Staff and Chief of Naval Operations.

Some time before this edifying seminar was adjourned for lunch, Marshall, having parted from his horse and scrubbed himself in the shower, turned up at his office, where he found the "pilot message," the fourteen parts, and the one o'clock delivery message all awaiting his attention. After considering these intercepts, with General Gerow, General Miles, and Colonel Bratton, among others, contributing to their elucidation, Marshall professed to see "some definite significance" pointing to the fact that "something was going to happen at 1 o'clock." He then drafted a dispatch to General [Walter] Short in Hawaii and to other Pacific outposts. This message read:

"The Japanese are presenting at 1 P.M. Eastern Standard Time, today, what appears to be an ultimatum. Also they are under orders to destroy their code machine immediately. Just what significance the hour set may have we do not know, but be on alert accordingly."

Marshall informed Stark of his intention to dispatch this message. Stark put up the phone, thought it over, and then called Marshall back, requesting him to have the message transmitted to naval commanders in the Pacific. Marshall added the instruction.

The Chief of Staff completed this message at 11:58 A.M., one hour and twenty-seven minutes before the Japanese attack on Pearl Harbor. It was typed for clarity, encoded, and finally sent off by commercial radio. The explanation for this decision was that the Army radio in Hawaii had been having difficulty that morning communicating with the War Department. But Marshall knew that the time was short. The FBI radio was available. When he talked with Stark, the Admiral volunteered the use of the powerful Navy transmitter. Above all, there was on Marshall's desk a scrambler telephone by which he could have reached Hawaii in a matter of minutes. He refrained from using it, he said, because of the "possibility of a leak which would embarrass the State Department." How the State Department could be embarrassed to any greater degree than by having Mr. Hull's diplomacy rewarded with war, and what conceivable effect the embarrassment would have had on negotiations already broken off, are matters which General Marshall may be able to explain, but which elude normal processes of ratiocination.

The message reached Honolulu at 7:33 A.M. and was being carried through the streets by a bicycle messenger when the first Japanese bombs began to drop. It was delivered to the signal office of the Hawaiian Department of the Army at 11:45 A.M., two hours after the last Japanese plane had retired, and, because it was not marked "Priority" or "Urgent," as were other waiting coded messages, it was laid aside and not decoded until 2:58 P.M., seven hours and three minutes after the attack. It finally reached the hands of General Short eight hours and twelve minutes after being filed for transmission.

At 7:55 A.M., the Japanese carrier planes, having received no word from Tokyo to withhold their attack because of a successful outcome of negotiations with the United States, struck the fleet at Pearl Harbor and Army and Navy air fields on Oahu. The surprise was complete. Eight American battleships and several smaller naval vessels were knocked out, most of the Army planes were destroyed on the ground, and 2,326 soldiers, sailors, and marines were killed. Japan lost a relatively small number of planes and a few midget submarines.

All wartime and immediate postwar discussions of the surprise of the United States at Pearl Harbor reached the conclusion that one or another individual or group was responsible for the disaster. In 1962, ROBERTA WOHLSTETTER published *Pearl Harbor: Warning and Decision,* a study in depth of American intelligence operations before December 7, 1941. The recipient of a Bancroft prize in American history for her careful work, Wohlstetter seeks neither to condemn nor to indict but rather to explain how the whole government shared in the failure to anticipate an attack on Pearl Harbor.*

Roberta Wohlstetter

Pearl Harbor:
A Failure to Anticipate

If our intelligence system and all our other channels of information failed to produce an accurate image of Japanese intentions and capabilities, it was not for want of the relevant materials. Never before have we had so complete an intelligence picture of the enemy. And perhaps never again will we have such a magnificent collection of sources at our disposal.

To review these sources briefly, an American cryptanalyst, Col. William F. Friedman, had broken the top-priority Japanese diplomatic code, which enabled us to listen to a large proportion of the privileged communications between Tokyo and the major Japanese embassies throughout the world. Not only did we know in advance how the Japanese ambassadors in Washing-

ton were advised, and how much they were instructed to say, but we also were listening to top-secret messages on the Tokyo-Berlin and Tokyo-Rome circuits, which gave us information vital for conduct of the war in the Atlantic and Europe. In the Far East this source provided minute details on movements connected with the Japanese program of expansion into Southeast Asia.

Besides the strictly diplomatic codes, our cryptanalysts also had some success in reading codes used by Japanese agents in major American and foreign ports. Those who were on the distribution list for MAGIC had access to much of what these agents were reporting to Tokyo and what Tokyo was demanding of them in the Panama Canal Zone, in cities along the east and

*Reprinted from *Pearl Harbor: Warning and Decision* by Roberta Wohlstetter with the permission of the publishers, Stanford University Press. © 1962 by the Board of Trustees of the Leland Stanford Junior University. Pp. 382–396. Footnote omitted.

west coasts of the Americas from northern Canada as far south as Brazil, and in ports throughout the Far East, including the Philippines and the Hawaiian Islands. They could determine what installations, what troop and ship movements, and what alert and defense measures were of interest to Tokyo at these points on the globe, as well as approximately how much correct information her agents were sending her.

Our naval leaders also had at their disposal the results of radio traffic analysis. While before the war our naval radio experts could not read the content of any Japanese naval or military coded messages, they were able to deduce from a study of intercepted ship call signs the composition and location of the Japanese Fleet units. After a change in call signs, they might lose sight of some units, and units that went into port in home waters were also lost because the ships in port used frequencies that our radios were unable to intercept. Most of the time, however, our traffic analysts had the various Japanese Fleet units accurately pinpointed on our naval maps.

Extremely competent on-the-spot economic and political analysis was furnished by Ambassador Grew and his staff in Tokyo. Ambassador Grew was himself a most sensitive and accurate observer, as evidenced by his dispatches to the State Department. His observations were supported and supplemented with military detail by frequent reports from American naval attachés and observers in key Far Eastern ports. Navy Intelligence had men with radio equipment located along the coast of China, for example, who reported the convoy movements toward Indochina. There were also naval observers stationed in various high-tension areas in Thailand and Indochina who could fill in the local outlines of Japanese political intrigue and military planning. In Tokyo and other Japanese cities, it

is true, Japanese censorship grew more and more rigid during 1941, until Ambassador Grew felt it necessary to disclaim any responsibility for noting or reporting overt military evidence of an imminent outbreak of war. This careful Japanese censorship naturally cut down visual confirmation of the decoded information but very probably never achieved the opaqueness of Russia's Iron Curtain.

During this period the data and interpretations of British intelligence were also available to American officers in Washington and the Far East, though the British and Americans tended to distrust each other's privileged information.

In addition to secret sources, there were some excellent public ones. Foreign correspondents for *The New York Times, The Herald Tribune,* and *The Washington Post* were stationed in Tokyo and Shanghai and in Canberra, Australia. Their reporting as well as their predictions on the Japanese political scene were on a very high level. Frequently their access to news was more rapid and their judgment of its significance as reliable as that of our Intelligence officers. This was certainly the case for 1940 and most of 1941. For the last few weeks before the Pearl Harbor strike, however, the public newspaper accounts were not very useful. It was necessary to have secret information in order to know what was happening. Both Tokyo and Washington exercised very tight control over leaks during this crucial period, and the newsmen accordingly had to limit their accounts to speculation and notices of diplomatic meetings with no exact indication of the content of the diplomatic exchanges.

The Japanese press was another important public source. During 1941 it proclaimed with increasing shrillness the Japanese government's determination to pursue its program of expansion into Southeast Asia and the desire of the military to clear the Far East of British and American colonial exploitation. This particular source was rife with explicit signals of aggressive intent.

Finally, an essential part of the intelligence picture for 1941 was both public and privileged information on American policy and activities in the Far East. During the year the pattern of action and interaction between the Japanese and American governments grew more and more complex. At the last, it became especially important for anyone charged with the responsibility of ordering an alert to know what moves the American government was going to make with respect to Japan, as well as to try to guess what Japan's next move would be, since Japan's next move would respond in part to ours. Unfortunately our military leaders, and especially our Intelligence officers, were sometimes as surprised as the Japanese at the moves of the White House and the State Department. They usually had more orderly anticipations about Japanese policy and conduct than they had about America's. On the other hand, it was also true that State Department and White House officials were handicapped in judging Japanese intentions and estimates of risk by an inadequate picture of our own military vulnerability.

All of the public and private sources of information mentioned were available to America's political and military leaders in 1941. It is only fair to remark, however, that no single person or agency ever had at any given moment all the signals existing in this vast information network. The signals lay scattered in a number of different agencies; some were decoded, some were not; some traveled through rapid channels of communication, some were blocked by technical or procedural delays; some never reached a center of decision. But it is legitimate to review again the general sort of picture that emerged during the first week

of December from the signals readily at hand. Anyone close to President Roosevelt was likely to have before him the following significant fragments.

There was first of all a picture of gathering troop and ship movements down the China coast and into Indochina. The large dimensions of this movement to the south were established publicly and visually as well as by analysis of ship call signs. Two changes in Japanese naval call signs—one on November 1 and another on December 1—had also been evaluated by Naval Intelligence as extremely unusual and as signs of major preparations for some sort of Japanese offensive. The two changes had interfered with the speed of American radio traffic analysis. Thousands of interceptions after December 1 were necessary before the new call signs could be read. Partly for this reason American radio analysts disagreed about the locations of the Japanese carriers. One group held that all the carriers were near Japan because they had not been able to identify a carrier call sign since the middle of November. Another group believed that they had located one carrier division in the Marshalls. The probability seemed to be that the carriers, wherever they were, had gone into radio silence; and past experience led the analysts to believe that they were therefore in waters near the Japanese homeland, where they could communicate with each other on wavelengths that we could not intercept. However, our inability to locate the carriers exactly, combined with the two changes in call signs, was itself a danger signal.

Our best secret source, MAGIC, was confirming the aggressive intentions of the new military cabinet in Tokyo, which had replaced the last moderate cabinet on October 17. In particular, MAGIC provided details of some of the preparations for the move into Southeast Asia. Running counter to this were increased troop shipments to the Manchurian border in October. (The intelligence picture is never clear-cut.) But withdrawals had begun toward the end of that month. MAGIC also carried explicit instructions to the Japanese ambassadors in Washington to pursue diplomatic negotiations with the United States with increasing energy, but at the same time it announced a deadline for the favorable conclusion of the negotiations, first for November 25, later postponed until November 29. In case of diplomatic failure by that date, the Japanese ambassadors were told, Japanese patience would be exhausted, Japan was determined to pursue her Greater East Asia policy, and on November 29 "things" would automatically begin to happen.

On November 26 Secretary Hull rejected Japan's latest bid for American approval of her policies in China and Indochina. MAGIC had repeatedly characterized this Japanese overture as the "last," and it now revealed the ambassadors' reaction of consternation and despair over the American refusal and also their country's characterization of the American Ten Point Note as an "ultimatum."

On the basis of this collection of signals, Army and Navy Intelligence experts in Washington tentatively placed D-day *for the Japanese Southeastern campaign* during the week end of November 30, and when this failed to materialize, during the week end of December 7. They also compiled an accurate list of probable British and Dutch targets and included the Philippines and Guam as possible American targets.

Also available in this mass of information, but long forgotten, was a rumor reported by Ambassador Grew in January, 1941. It came from what was regarded as a not-very-reliable source, the Peruvian embassy, and stated that the Japanese were preparing a surprise air attack on Pearl Harbor. Curiously the date of the report is coincident roughly with what we now know to have been the date of inception of [Admiral] Yamamoto's plan; but the coincidence is fairly pure. The rumor was traced to a Japanese cook in the Embassy who had been reading a novel that began with an attack on Pearl Harbor. Consequently everyone concerned, including Ambassador Grew, labeled the rumor as quite fantastic and the plan as absurdly impossible. American judgment was consistent with Japanese judgment at this time, since Yamamoto's plan was in direct contradiction to Japanese naval tactical doctrine.

On the basis of this rapid recapitulation of the highlights in the signal picture, it is apparent that our decisionmakers had at hand an impressive amount of information on the enemy. They did not have the complete list of targets, since none of the last-minute estimates included Pearl Harbor. They did not know the exact hour and date for opening the attack. They did not have an accurate knowledge of Japanese capabilities or of Japanese ability to accept very high risks. The crucial question then, we repeat, is, If we could enumerate accurately the British and Dutch targets and give credence to a Japanese attack against them either on November 30 or December 7, why were we not expecting a specific danger to *ourselves?* And by the word "expecting," we mean expecting in the sense of taking specific alert actions to meet the contingencies of attack by land, sea, or air.

There are several answers to this question that have become apparent in the course of this study. First of all, it is much easier *after* the event to sort the relevant from the irrelevant signals. After the event, of course, a signal is always crystal clear; we can now see what disaster it was signaling, since the disaster has occurred. But before the event it is obscure and pregnant with conflicting meanings. It comes to the observer embedded in an atmosphere of "noise," i.e., in the company of all sorts of information that is useless and irrelevant for predicting the particular disaster. For example, in Washington, Pearl Harbor signals were competing with a vast number of signals from the European theater. These European signals announced danger more frequently and more specifically than any coming from the Far East. The Far Eastern signals were also arriving at a center of decision where they had to compete with the prevailing belief that an unprotected offensive force acts as a deterrent rather than a target. In Honolulu they were competing *not* with signals from the European theater, but rather with a large number of signals announcing Japanese intentions and preparations to attack Soviet Russia rather than to move southward; here they were also competing with expectations of local sabotage prepared by previous alert situations.

In short, we failed to anticipate Pearl Harbor not for want of the relevant materials, but because of a plethora of irrelevant ones. Much of the appearance of wanton neglect that emerged in various investigations of the disaster resulted from the unconscious suppression of vast congeries of signs pointing in every direction except Pearl Harbor. It was difficult later to recall these signs since they had led nowhere. Signals that are characterized today as absolutely unequivocal warnings of surprise air attack on Pearl Harbor become, on analysis in the context of December, 1941, not merely ambiguous but occasionally inconsistent with such an attack. . . .

There is a difference, then, between having a signal available somewhere in the heap of irrelevancies, and perceiving it as a warning; and there is also a difference between perceiving it as a warning, and acting or getting action on it. These distinctions, simple as they are, illuminate the obscurity shrouding this moment in history. . . .

To illustrate the difference between having and perceiving a signal, let us . . . [refer] to Colonel Fielder. . . . Though he was an untrained and inexperienced Intelligence officer, he headed Army Intelligence at Pearl Harbor at the time of the attack. He had been on the job for only four months, and he regarded as quite satisfactory his sources of information and his contacts with the Navy locally and with Army Intelligence in Washington. Evidently he was unaware that Army Intelligence in Washington was not allowed to send him any "action" or policy information, and he was therefore not especially concerned about trying to read beyond the obvious meaning of any given communication that came under his eyes. Colonel Bratton, head of Army Far Eastern Intelligence in Washington, however, had a somewhat more realistic view of the extent of Colonel Fielder's knowledge. At the end of November, Colonel Bratton had learned about the [Japanese] winds-code setup [signaling possible breaks in diplomatic relations] and was also apprised that the naval traffic analysis unit under Commander Rochefort in Honolulu was monitoring 24 hours a day for an execute. He was understandably worried about the lack of communication between this unit and Colonel Fielder's office, and by December 5 he finally felt that the matter was urgent enough to warrant sending a message directly to Colonel Fielder about the winds code. Now any information on the winds code, since it belonged to the highest classification of secret information, and since it was therefore automatically evaluated as "action" information, could not be sent through normal G-2 channels. Colonel Bratton had to figure out another way to get the information to Colonel Fielder. He sent this message: "Contact Commander Rochefort immediately thru Commandant Fourteenth Naval District regarding broadcasts from Tokyo reference weather." Signal Corps records establish that Colonel Fielder received this message. How did he react to it? He filed it. According to his testimony in 1945, it made no impression on him and he did not attempt to see Rochefort. He could not sense any urgency behind the lines because he was not expecting immediate trouble, and his expectations determined what he read. A warning signal was available to him, but he did not perceive it.

Colonel Fielder's lack of experience may make this example seem to be an exception. So let us recall the performance of Captain Wilkinson, the naval officer who headed the Office of Naval Intelligence in Washington in the fall of 1941 and who is unanimously acclaimed for a distinguished and brilliant career. His treatment of a now-famous Pearl Harbor signal does not sound much different in the telling. After the event, the signal in question was labeled "the bomb-plot message." It originated in Tokyo on September 24 and was sent to an agent in Honolulu. It requested the agent to divide Pearl Harbor into five areas and to make his future reports on ships in harbor with reference to those areas. Tokyo was especially interested in the locations of battleships, destroyers, and carriers, and also in any information on the mooring of more than one ship at a single dock.

This message was decoded and translated on October 9 and shortly thereafter distributed to Army, Navy, and State Department recipients of MAGIC. Commander Kramer, a naval expert on MAGIC, had marked the message with an asterisk, signifying that he thought it to be of particular interest. But what was its interest? Both he

and Wilkinson agreed that it illustrated the "nicety" of Japanese intelligence, the incredible zeal and efficiency with which they collected detail. The division into areas was interpreted as a device for shortening the reports. Admiral Stark was similarly impressed with Japanese efficiency, and no one felt it necessary to forward the message to Admiral Kimmel. No one read into it a specific danger to ships anchored in Pearl Harbor. At the time, this was a reasonable estimate, since somewhat similar requests for information were going to Japanese agents in Panama, Vancouver, Portland, San Diego, San Francisco, and other places. It should be observed, however, that the estimate was reasonable only on the basis of a very rough check on the quantity of espionage messages passing between Tokyo and these American ports. No one in Far Eastern Intelligence had subjected the messages to any more refined analysis. An observer assigned to such a job would have been able to record an increase in the frequency and specificity of Tokyo's requests concerning Manila and Pearl Harbor in the last weeks before the outbreak of war, and he would have noted that Tokyo was not displaying the same interest in other American ports. These observations, while not significant in isolation, might have been useful in the general signal picture.

There is no need, however, to confine our examples to Intelligence personnel. Indeed, the crucial areas where the signals failed to communicate a warning were in the operational branches of the armed services. Let us take Admiral Kimmel and his reaction to the information that the Japanese were destroying most of their codes in major Far Eastern consulates and also in London and Washington. Since the Pearl Harbor attack, this information has frequently been characterized by military experts who were not stationed in Honolulu as an "unmistakable tip-off." As Admiral Ingersoll explained at the congressional hearings, with the lucidity characteristic of statements after the event:

If you rupture diplomatic negotiations you do not necessarily have to burn your codes. The diplomats go home and they can pack up their codes with their dolls and take them home. Also, when you rupture diplomatic negotiations, you do not rupture consular relations. The consuls stay on.

Now, in this particular set of dispatches that did not mean a rupture of diplomatic negotiations, it meant war, and that information was sent out to the fleets as soon as we got it. . . .

The phrase "it meant war" was, of course, pretty vague; war in Manila, Hong Kong, Singapore, and Batavia is not war 5000 miles away in Pearl Harbor. Before the event, for Admiral Kimmel, code burning in major Japanese consulates in the Far East may have "meant war," but it did not signal danger of an air attack on Pearl Harbor. In the first place, the information that he received was not the original MAGIC. He learned from Washington that Japanese consulates were burning "almost all" of their codes, not all of them, and Honolulu was not included on the list. He knew from a local source that the Japanese consulate in Honolulu was burning secret papers (not necessarily codes), and this back yard burning had happened three or four times during the year. In July, 1941, Kimmel had been informed that the Japanese consulates in lands neighboring Indochina had destroyed codes, and he interpreted the code burning in December as a similar attempt to protect codes in case the Americans or their British and Dutch allies tried to seize the consulates in reprisal for the southern advance. This also was a reasonable interpretation at the time, though not an especially keen one.

Indeed, at the time there was a good deal of evidence available to support all the wrong interpretations of the last-minute signals, and the interpretations appeared wrong only *after* the event. There was, for example, a good deal of evidence to support the hypothesis that Japan would attack the Soviet Union from the east while the Russian Army was heavily engaged in the west. Admiral Turner, head of Navy War Plans in Washington, was an enthusiastic adherent of this view and argued the high probability of a Japanese attack on Russia up until the last week in November, when he had to concede that most of Japan's men and supplies were moving south. Richard Sorge, the expert Soviet spy who had direct access to the Japanese Cabinet, had correctly predicted the southern move as early as July, 1941, but even he was deeply alarmed during September and early October by the large number of troop movements to the Manchurian border. He feared that his July advice to the Soviet Union had been in error, and his alarm ultimately led to his capture on October 14. For at this time he increased his radio messages to Moscow to the point where it was possible for the Japanese police to pinpoint the source of the broadcasts.

It is important to emphasize here that most of the men that we have cited in our examples, such as Captain Wilkinson and Admirals Turner and Kimmel—these men and their colleagues who were involved in the Pearl Harbor disaster—were as efficient and loyal a group of men as one could find. Some of them were exceptionally able and dedicated. The fact of surprise at Pearl Harbor has never been persuasively explained by accusing the participants, individually or in groups, of conspiracy or negligence or stupidity. What these examples illustrate is rather the very human tendency to pay attention to the signals that support current expectations about enemy behavior. If no one is listening for signals of an attack against a highly improbable target, then it is very difficult for the signals to be heard.

For every signal that came into the information net in 1941 there were usually several plausible alternative explanations, and it is not surprising that our observers and analysts were inclined to select the explanations that fitted the popular hypotheses. They sometimes set down new contradictory evidence side by side with existing hypotheses, and they also sometimes held two contradictory beliefs at the same time. ... This happen[ed] in G-2 estimates for the fall of 1941. Apparently human beings have a stubborn attachment to old beliefs and an equally stubborn resistance to new material that will upset them.

Besides the tendency to select whatever was in accord with one's expectations, there were many other blocks to perception that prevented our analysts from making the correct interpretation. We have just mentioned the masses of conflicting evidence that supported alternative and equally reasonable hypotheses. This is the phenomenon of noise in which a signal is embedded. Even at its normal level, noise presents problems in distraction; but in addition to the natural clatter of useless information and competing signals, in 1941 a number of factors combined to raise the usual noise level. First of all, it had been raised, especially in Honolulu, by the background of previous alert situations and false alarms. Earlier alerts, as we have seen, had centered attention on local sabotage and on signals supporting the hypothesis of a probable Japanese attack on Russia. Second, in both Honolulu and Washington, individual reactions to danger had been numbed, or at least dulled, by the continuous international tension.

A third factor that served to increase the natural noise level was the positive effort made by the enemy to keep the relevant signals quiet. The Japanese security system was an important and successful block to perception. It was able to keep the strictest cloak of secrecy around the Pearl Harbor attack and to limit knowledge only to those closely associated with the details of military and naval planning. In the Japanese Cabinet only the Navy Minister and the Army Minister (who was also Prime Minister) knew of the plan before the task force left its final port of departure.

In addition to keeping certain signals quiet, the enemy tried to create noise, and sent false signals into our information system by carrying on elaborate "spoofs." False radio traffic made us believe that certain ships were maneuvering near the mainland of Japan. The Japanese also sent to individual commanders false war plans for Chinese targets, which were changed only at the last moment to bring them into line with the Southeastern movement.

A fifth barrier to accurate perception was the fact that the relevant signals were subject to change, often very sudden change. This was true even of the so-called static intelligence, which included data on capabilities and the composition of military forces. In the case of our 1941 estimates of the infeasibility of torpedo attacks in the shallow waters of Pearl Harbor, or the underestimation of the range and performance of the Japanese Zero, the changes happened too quickly to appear in an intelligence estimate.

Sixth, our own security system sometimes prevented the communication of signals. It confronted our officers with the problem of trying to keep information from the enemy without keeping it from each other, and, as in the case of MAGIC, they were not always successful. As we have seen, only a very few key individuals saw these secret messages, and they saw them only briefly. They had no opportunity or time to make a critical review of the material, and each one assumed that others who had seen it would arrive at identical interpretations. Exactly who those "others" were was not quite clear to any recipient. Admiral Stark, for example, thought Admiral Kimmel was reading all of MAGIC. Those who were not on the list of recipients, but who had learned somehow of the existence of the decodes, were sure that they contained military as well as diplomatic information and believed that the contents were much fuller and more precise than they actually were. The effect of carefully limiting the reading and discussion of MAGIC, which was certainly necessary to safeguard the secret of our knowledge of the code, was thus to reduce this group of signals to the point where they were scarcely heard.

To these barriers of noise and security we must add the fact that the necessarily precarious character of intelligence information and predictions was reflected in the wording of instructions to take action. The warning messages were somewhat vague and ambiguous. Enemy moves are often subject to reversal on short notice, and this was true for the Japanese. They had plans for canceling their attacks on American possessions in the Pacific up to 24 hours before the time set for attack. A full alert in the Hawaiian Islands, for example, was one condition that might have caused the Pearl Harbor task force to return to Japan on December 5 or 6. The fact that intelligence predictions must be based on moves that are almost always reversible makes understandable the reluctance of the intelligence analyst to make bold assertions. Even if he is willing to risk his reputation on a firm prediction of attack at a definite time and place, no commander will in turn lightly risk the pen-

alties and costs of a full alert. In December, 1941, a full alert required shooting down any unidentified aircraft sighted over the Hawaiian Islands. Yet this might have been interpreted by Japan as the first overt act. At least that was one consideration that influenced General Short to order his lowest degree of alert. While the cautious phrasing in the messages to the theater is certainly understandable, it nevertheless constituted another block on the road to perception. The sentences in the final theater warnings—"A surprise aggressive move in any direction is a possibility" and "Japanese future action unpredictable but hostile action possible at any moment"—could scarcely have been expected to inform the theater commanders of any change in their strategic situation.

Last but not least we must also mention the blocks to perception and communication inherent in any large bureaucratic organization, and those that stemmed from intraservice and interservice rivalries. The most glaring example of rivalry in the Pearl Harbor case was that between Naval War Plans and Naval Intelligence. A general prejudice against intellectuals and specialists, not confined to the military but unfortunately widely held in America, also made it difficult for intelligence experts to be heard. McCollum, Bratton, Sadtler, and a few others who felt that the signal picture was ominous enough to warrant more urgent warnings had no power to influence decision. The Far Eastern code analysts, for example, were believed to be too immersed in the "Oriental point of view." Low budgets for American Intelligence departments reflected the low prestige of this activity, whereas in England, Germany, and Japan, 1941 budgets reached a height that was regarded by the American Congress as quite beyond reason.

In view of all these limitations to perception and communication, is the fact of surprise at Pearl Harbor, then, really so surprising? Even with these limitations explicitly recognized, there remains the step between perception and action. Let us assume that the first hurdle has been crossed: An available signal has been perceived as an indication of imminent danger. Then how do we resolve the next questions: What specific danger is the signal trying to communicate, and what specific action or preparation should follow?

On November 27, General MacArthur had received a war warning very similar to the one received by General Short in Honolulu. MacArthur's response had been promptly translated into orders designed to protect his bombers from possible air attack from Formosan land bases. But the orders were carried out very slowly. By December 8, Philippine time, only half of the bombers ordered to the south had left the Manila area, and reconnaissance over Formosa had not been undertaken. There was no sense of urgency in preparing for a Japanese air attack, partly because our intelligence estimates had calculated that the Japanese aircraft did not have sufficient range to bomb Manila from Formosa.

The information that Pearl Harbor had been attacked arrived at Manila early in the morning of December 8, giving the Philippine forces some 9 or 10 hours to prepare for an attack. But did an air attack on Pearl Harbor necessarily mean that the Japanese would strike from the air at the Philippines? Did they have enough equipment to mount both air attacks successfully? Would they come from Formosa or from carriers? Intelligence had indicated that they would have to come from carriers, yet the carriers were evidently off Hawaii. MacArthur's headquarters also pointed out that there had been no formal declaration of war against Japan by the United States. Therefore approval could not be granted for a counterattack on Formosan bases. Furthermore there were technical disagreements among airmen as to whether a counterattack should be mounted without advance photographic reconnaissance. While Brereton was arranging permission to undertake photographic reconnaissance, there was further disagreement about what to do with the aircraft in the meantime. Should they be sent aloft or should they be dispersed to avoid destruction in case the Japanese reached the airfields? When the Japanese bombers arrived shortly after noon, they found all the American aircraft wingtip to wingtip on the ground. Even the signal of an actual attack on Pearl Harbor was not an unambiguous signal of an attack on the Philippines, and it did not make clear what response was best.

CHESTER WILMOT (1911–1954), the Australian journalist and military historian whose chief work was a military-diplomatic history of World War II, *The Struggle for Europe* (1952), describes Roosevelt's and Hull's wartime leadership as an outgrowth of the traditional aversion of the United States to colonialism and balance-of-power diplomacy. It is Wilmot's conclusion that such a strategy did not contain a realistic estimate of either Russian or British attitudes toward international affairs. Does Wilmot's failure to take account of the shortcomings of the old balance-of-power diplomacy and of domestic pressures on the Roosevelt administration make American policy seem excessively naïve?*

Chester Wilmot

A Naïve Attempt to End Spheres of Influence

The impending collapse of the Allied coalition now became one of [Propaganda Minister Joseph] Goebbels's favourite themes. On September 4, 1944, his spokesman told a press conference in Berlin, "The reports of Soviet victories in the Balkans will surely not be pleasant to the English. . . . With the apparent approach of victory for the Allies it is certain that the political conflicts will increase and will one day cause the edifice of our enemies to break irreparably." This expectation was not altogether illogical. Since the sixteenth century the abiding purpose of British foreign policy had been to maintain the balance of power in Europe. To prevent the domination of the Continent by one power or another, the British had fought half a dozen major wars, and in the last hundred years they had been almost equally determined to ensure that Russia did not gain control of the Black Sea Straits and the Bosphorus.

Both these dangers had arisen again, and acutely, with the Red Army's advance into Poland and Rumania, and it was becoming clearer every day that the annihilation of Germany would leave the Soviet Union in command of Central and South-Eastern Europe. Thus it was not unreasonable for Hitler and Goebbels to believe that this prospect would create friction between Russia and Britain, especially in the Balkans, and would weaken the British resolve to enforce the demand for Germany's unconditional surrender. The Germans

*Reprinted from pp. 446–448, 632–638, *The Struggle for Europe* by Chester Wilmot. Copyright 1952 by Chester Wilmot. Reprinted by permission of Harper & Row, Publishers, and Harold Matson Company, Inc. Some footnotes omitted.

were right in suspecting that Churchill was disturbed by the recent developments in Eastern Europe, but they did not realise the extent to which the strategy and diplomacy of the Western Allies were governed by Roosevelt's determination to keep out of the Balkans.

Before the Teheran Conference [in 1943] . . . the President's attitude to all British proposals for operations against Southern Europe had been governed by his belief that the quickest and cheapest road to military victory lay through Western France. At the end of the first day in Teheran he had said to his son, Elliott, "I see no reason for putting the lives of American soldiers in jeopardy in order to protect real or fancied British interests on the European continent. We are at war and our job is to win it as fast as possible, and without adventures."[1] Operations in the Balkans, presumably, came under the heading of "adventures."

By the end of this conference Roosevelt had long-term reasons for wishing to keep out of South-Eastern Europe. He wanted to make certain of Russia's promised participation in the war against Japan and in the establishment of the United Nations. Accordingly, he was determined to avoid any action which might make Stalin suspicious of Anglo-American intentions, for he realised that the pursuit of an independent course by Russia would be as disastrous for the United Nations as American Isolation had been for the League. It is apparent from the [Harry] Hopkins Papers and from Cordell Hull's Memoirs that Roosevelt became aware of Soviet ambitions, but hoped that, if Russia could be guaranteed security within the United Nations, she would not seek to protect herself by the creation of spheres of influence beyond her frontiers.

Far from being anxious, as was Churchill, to re-establish Western influence and prestige in Central and South-Eastern Europe, Roosevelt feared that any Anglo-American move in that direction would estrange the Russians and lead them to set up a *cordon sanitaire* of satellite states. Both Roosevelt and Hull were opposed in principle to all "spheres of influence," other than that of the United States in the Americas. Hull believed that "any creation of zones of influence would inevitably sow the seeds of future conflict . . . [and] could not but derogate from the overall authority of the international security organisation."[2] This doctrine may have been sound in theory, but it provided no answer to the practical danger that, unless some immediate limits were set by the Western Powers, Stalin would establish Russia's hegemony over much of Europe before the international security organisation could be established.

Churchill knew that there could be no stability or harmony on the Continent, if the advantage of power lay overwhelmingly with Russia, but Roosevelt believed that this problem could be solved by an extension of the "Good Neighbour" policy which he had applied with such success in the Western Hemisphere. His views appear to have been summed up in a memorandum prepared by the U.S. War Department before the Quebec Conference of August 1943. This paper said, "Since Russia is the decisive factor in the war, she must be given every assistance and every effort must be made to obtain her friendship. Since without question she will dominate Europe on the defeat of the Axis, it is even more essential to develop and maintain the most friendly relations with Russia."[3] Roosevelt apparently accepted al-

---

[1] Elliott Roosevelt, *As He Saw It*, p. 186.

[2] Hull, [*Memoirs*] p. 1,452.

[3] Quoted by Sherwood, [*Roosevelt and Hopkins*] p. 748.

most with equanimity the prospect of Russia dominating the Continent, since he genuinely believed that friendliness and frankness on his part would be met by an equally sympathetic response from Stalin. . . .

En route to the Crimea [in February 1945], Roosevelt and Churchill held a brief preliminary conference at Malta, where they discussed the Yalta agenda and those issues which had introduced a certain acrimony into their relationship since their last meeting at Quebec in September, [1944]. From these discussions Churchill hoped that there would emerge a common policy which he and the President could then present to Stalin and by their unity offset the advantage of his strength. It was apparent, however, that Roosevelt was as anxious as ever to avoid making commitments or giving the Russians any reason to think that they were dealing with an Anglo-American alliance. He saw himself as "the Good Neighbour of the World," the independent arbiter whose task it was to preserve harmony between Churchill and Stalin and to prevent Anglo-Soviet rivalry from causing a breach in "Big Three Unity." In the course of the Malta meeting the British delegation were dismayed to find that their American colleagues were less suspicious of Russia's post-war intentions than they were of Britain's. . . .

The roots of this suspicion lay deep in history. Ever since 1776, Americans have nurtured a profound prejudice against "colonialism," and have tended to presume that the independence which brought them such benefits must likewise transform the lives of peoples less fortunate than themselves. With little regard for the merits, or the difficulties, of particular cases, they have consistently favoured the early grant of self-government to all dependent peoples, and particularly to those

still under the dominion of the British Crown, for to Americans—by virtue of their past—Britain has remained the symbol of all Imperialism. Although ready to concede that British colonial policies were more progressive and more humane than those of any other country, they persisted in the belief that Imperial rule contained such inherent evils that even good empires must be bad.

This American belief did not imply any weakening of the traditional bonds of common heritage and mutual interest which preserved the essential unity of the English-speaking world, nor any lessening of the ties of almost filial affection which bound the United States to England. It was a case of the enlightened son seeking to reform the wayward father. In 1940, when Britain stood in danger of annihilation by a more sinister imperialism, the American people, under Roosevelt's leadership, gladly and generously came to her rescue, bringing material aid and moral encouragement not out of mere self-interest but from the realisation that, for all her shortcomings, Britain was the essential bulwark of freedom, the last unconquered trustee of Western civilisation in Europe. Yet there was always a reservation in the American readiness to help. Roosevelt was determined to prevent the destruction of England, but he was equally determined that American aid should not be used to bolster up the British Empire. With him the inborn American prejudice against Imperialism assumed the force of a principle, and he saw, in the fluidity of the world situation brought about by war, the opportunity for extending throughout the colonial world the revolution that had started in 1776.

Roosevelt's "assault" upon the colonial concept began with the Atlantic Charter. The first draft of this declaration was drawn up by Churchill, who endeavoured to set forth the principles which should guide the democratic nations in their struggle against German aggression and in the re-establishment of European peace. Reporting to the House of Commons on September 9th, 1941, the Prime Minister said: "At the Atlantic meeting we had in mind the restoration of the sovereignty . . . of the states . . . now under the Nazi yoke." This, he insisted, was "quite a separate problem from the progressive evolution of self-governing institutions in the regions and peoples that owe allegiance to the British Crown."

The President, on the other hand, had no such limited view. During the "Atlantic Charter Conference" he told Churchill: "I can't believe that we can fight a war against fascist slavery, and at the same time not work to free people all over the world from a backward colonial policy. . . . The peace cannot include any continued despotism. The structure of peace demands and will get equality of peoples. Equality of peoples involves the utmost freedom of competitive trade."[4] Thus, when he added to Churchill's draft the statement that he and the Prime Minister wished to "see sovereign rights and self-government restored to those who have been forcibly deprived of them," Roosevelt was thinking not only of the occupied countries of Europe but also of colonial peoples throughout the world. Furthermore, when he inserted an article declaring that they would endeavour "without discrimination to further the enjoyment by all states, great or small, victor or vanquished, of access, on equal terms, to the trade and to the raw materials of the world," the President was avowedly aiming at the Ottawa Agreements, the foundation of Imperial Preference. Appreciating this, Churchill demanded that the words "without dis-

crimination" should be replaced by the phrase "with due respect to their existing obligations," but this gained him only a brief respite from American pressure.

Five months later, when the master Lend-Lease Agreement was signed, Roosevelt insisted that, in return for American aid, Britain must agree to "the elimination of all forms of discriminatory treatment in international commerce and the reduction of tariffs and trade barriers" after the war. Cordell Hull, the prime advocate of this clause, reports that "a few Tory members of the British Cabinet . . . regarded the Lend-Lease Agreement . . . as an attempt to infringe on British Imperial sovereignty"[5]—which, of course, it was.

In his Memoirs Hull is quite frank about the President's purpose. "We had," he writes, "definite ideas with respect to the future of the British Colonial Empire, on which we differed with the British. It might be said that the future of that Empire was no business of ours; but we felt that unless dependent peoples were assisted toward ultimate self-government and were given it . . . they would provide kernels of conflict."[6] Neither Hull nor Roosevelt were content with the official British explanation that "self-government should be achieved within the British Commonwealth." On one occasion the President told his son, Elliott, "I've tried to make it clear to Winston—and the others—that, while we're their allies and in it to victory by their side, they must never get the idea that we're in it just to help them hang on to the archaic, medieval Empire ideas . . . Great Britain signed the Atlantic Charter. I hope they realize the United States government means to make them live up to it."[7]

4 Elliott Roosevelt, *As He Saw It*, p. 37.

5 Hull, op. cit., p. 1151.
6 Ibid., pp. 1477-8.
7 Elliott Roosevelt, op. cit., pp. 121-2.

Roosevelt's determination to make the Charter apply to colonial territories was reinforced by Japan's conquest of virtually all the British, Dutch and French colonies in the Far East. The failure of those powers to defend their possessions and the realisation that these would be liberated directly or indirectly by the military might of the United States greatly strengthened the President's hand. He saw the chance of insisting that these colonies would not be returned to their original owners, except in return for a guarantee that self-government, and eventually complete independence, would be granted to them.

There is no doubt that this was Roosevelt's policy. When Eden was in Washington in March 1943, "the President" (according to a memorandum written at the time by Hopkins) "made it clear that he did not want a commitment made in advance that all those colonies in the Far East should go back to the countries which owned or controlled them prior to the war." Hopkins also noted, "The President has once or twice urged the British to give up Hong Kong as a gesture of 'good will' ... Eden dryly remarked that he had not heard the President suggest any similar gestures on our own part." [8]

When Queen Wilhelmina saw Roosevelt later that year, he talked to her about the future of the Netherlands East Indies and, after reminding her that "it was American arms that would be liberating those colonies from the Japanese," he obtained a promise that the Indies would be granted "dominion status with the right of self-rule and equality." [9]

From Churchill, however, the President could extract no such assurance about British possessions, though he raised the question at nearly all their major meetings. In private Churchill replied, "Mr. President, I believe you are trying to do away with the British Empire," and in public he declared, "We mean to hold our own. I have not become the King's First Minister in order to preside over the liquidation of the British Empire." When Churchill made this statement—at the Mansion House on November 10th, 1942—few of his hearers realised that it was directed primarily at the man whom he was proud to acknowledge as "the greatest American friend we have ever known, and the greatest champion of freedom who has ever brought help and comfort from the new world to the old."

Undeterred by Churchill's defiant stand, Roosevelt continued to strive for the acceptance of his policy. Having set his heart on the establishment of an international organisation for the maintenance of peace, Roosevelt was the more determined to rid the world of "colonialism." He saw the issue in terms that were simple, almost naïve; and not always true. "The colonial system means war," he told Elliott. "Exploit the resources of an India, a Burma, a Java; take all the wealth out of those countries, but never put anything back into them, things like education, decent standards of living, minimum health requirements—all you're doing is storing up the kind of trouble that leads to war. All you're doing is negating the value of any kind of organisational structure for peace before it begins." [10]

Roosevelt's vision of the peace included not only the ending of the colonial system, but the abandonment of what he regarded as its essential concomitants, spheres of influence and regional balances of power. He expected, as Hull told Congress, that when the United Nations organisation was established there would "no longer be any need

[8] Quoted by Sherwood, op. cit., pp. 718-9.
[9] Elliott Roosevelt, op. cit., pp. 223-4.
[10] Ibid., p. 74

for spheres of influence, for alliances, for balance of power, or any other of the special arrangements through which, in the unhappy past, nations strove to safeguard their security or promote their interests."

This idealistic vision was not shared by Churchill who knew from long experience of European history that nations are less likely to succumb to the temptation of aggrandisement if their ambitions are restrained by a reasonable balance of power, and that such a balance could be preserved only by alliances and other "special arrangements." Churchill was by no means anti-Russian, but as early as October 1942 he had set down the view that "it would be a measureless disaster if Russian barbarism were to overlay the culture and independence of the ancient states of Europe." After Teheran, while continuing to work for Hitler's defeat and Stalin's friendship, he had become alive to the danger that the war would leave the Soviet Union in a position of overwhelming power which could be counter-balanced only by a strong British Empire, a firm Anglo-American alliance and a United States of Europe.

The prospect of a Russian advance deep into Central and South-Eastern Europe dismayed Churchill, and was one of the main reasons for his unflagging advocacy of those Balkan operations which Roosevelt and the American Chiefs of Staff so persistently vetoed. Thwarted in his desire to forestall Russia militarily, Churchill endeavoured to restrain her by striking a political bargain direct with the Kremlin. In the early summer of 1944, before the Red Army had made any serious inroad on the Balkans, the Prime Minister proposed to Stalin (without the President's knowledge) that the "controlling interest" in Rumania and Bulgaria should be exercised by the Soviet Union, and in Greece and Yugoslavia by Britain. When news of this proposal reached Washington, the secretive British

approach to Moscow was resented, and the plan was condemned by Hull on the ground that it amounted to "the division of the Balkans into spheres of influence." In reply Churchill argued that he was not proposing to carve up the Balkans, but that in the re-establishment of civil government "someone must play the hand" and that this should be done by the power responsible for military operations in each country. Roosevelt was not altogether satisfied, but he agreed to give the arrangement a three months' trial on the understanding that it would apply only to immediate problems and would not prejudice the post-war settlement. Nevertheless, the plan remained suspect in Washington, particularly as the President gave his consent to it without consulting, or even advising, his Secretary of State!

American suspicions were sharpened when Churchill, during his visit to Moscow in October 1944, "extended the arrangement still further, even reducing to percentages the relative degree of influence which Britain and Russia individually should have in specified Balkan countries." [11] Each of the major powers placed its own interpretation on this agreement. The Russians regarded it as a formal acknowledgment of their predominant role and interest in the Danube Basin. The British saw it as the recognition of the *fait accompli* in that region and were thankful to have preserved even a small voice in the affairs of the Danubian states and to have kept Russia out of Greece. In Churchill's opinion it was not a matter of dividing the Balkans between Britain and Russia, but of preventing the Soviet Union extending its sphere of influence over the whole peninsula. The Americans, on the other hand, considered the agreement a betrayal of the Atlantic Charter, a sinister scheme to further Britain's

[11] Hull, op. cit., p. 1458.

Imperial ambitions. In the State Department it was denounced as "Churchiavellian." . . .

It was most tragic that such suspicion and discord should have developed . . . for it seems to have led Roosevelt and some of his intimates to presume that the future threat to world peace and the independence of small nations would come not from Russia or international Communism, but from the old colonial powers, and particularly Britain. This peculiar aberration can be explained only if it is remembered that . . . Roosevelt did not believe that Stalin cherished any imperialistic aspirations.

A distinguished historian whose numerous writings include three volumes on *The Age of Roosevelt* (1957–1960), ARTHUR SCHLESINGER, JR. (b. 1917) is one of the foremost authorities on Franklin Roosevelt's Presidency. Unlike Wilmot, Schlesinger views American wartime diplomacy as a sensible expression of the universalist, or Wilsonian, approach to foreign affairs. In an essay on "The Origins of the Cold War" (1967), a part of which makes up the following selection, Schlesinger argues that Roosevelt followed a sound wartime policy based on domestic and international considerations which he would have found difficult to ignore.*

Arthur Schlesinger, Jr.

A Realistic Attempt to End Spheres of Influence

Peacemaking after the Second World War was not so much a tapestry as it was a hopelessly raveled and knotted mess of yarn. Yet, for purposes of clarity, it is essential to follow certain threads. One theme indispensable to an understanding of the Cold War is the contrast between two clashing views of world order: the "universalist" view, by which all nations shared a common interest in all the affairs of the world, and the "sphere-of-influence" view, by which each great power would be assured by the other great powers of an acknowledged predominance in its own area of special interest. The universalist view assumed that national security would be guaranteed by an international organization. The sphere-of-interest view as-

sumed that national security would be guaranteed by the balance of power. While in practice these views have by no means been incompatible (indeed, our shaky peace has been based on a combination of the two), in the abstract they involved sharp contradictions.

The tradition of American thought in these matters was universalist—*i.e.* Wilsonian. Roosevelt had been a member of Wilson's subcabinet; in 1920, as candidate for Vice President, he had campaigned for the League of Nations. It is true that, within Roosevelt's infinitely complex mind, Wilsonianism warred with the perception of vital strategic interests he had imbibed from Mahan. Moreover, his temperamental inclination to settle things with

*Arthur Schlesinger, Jr., "The Origins of the Cold War," reprinted by special permission from *Foreign Affairs* (October, 1967), 26–40. Copyright 1967 by the Council on Foreign Relations, Inc., New York.

fellow princes around the conference table led him to regard the Big Three—or Four—as trustees for the rest of the world. On occasion, as this narrative will show, he was beguiled into flirtation with the sphere-of-influence heresy. But in principle he believed in joint action and remained a Wilsonian. His hope for Yalta, as he told the Congress on his return, was that it would "spell the end of the system of unilateral action, the exclusive alliances, the spheres of influence, the balances of power, and all the other expedients that have been tried for centuries—and have always failed."

Whenever Roosevelt backslid, he had at his side that Wilsonian fundamentalist, Secretary of State Cordell Hull, to recall him to the pure faith. After his visit to Moscow in 1943, Hull characteristically said that, with the Declaration of Four Nations on General Security (in which America, Russia, Britain and China pledged "united action . . . for the organization and maintenance of peace and security"), "there will no longer be need for spheres of influence, for alliances, for balance of power, or any other of the special arrangements through which, in the unhappy past, the nations strove to safeguard their security or to promote their interests."

Remembering the corruption of the Wilsonian vision by the secret treaties of the First World War, Hull was determined to prevent any sphere-of-influence nonsense after the Second World War. He therefore fought all proposals to settle border questions while the war was still on and, excluded as he largely was from wartime diplomacy, poured his not inconsiderable moral energy and frustration into the promulgation of virtuous and spacious general principles.

In adopting the universalist view, Roosevelt and Hull were not indulging personal hobbies. Sumner Welles, Adolf Berle,

Averell Harriman, Charles Bohlen—all, if with a variety of nuances, opposed the sphere-of-influence approach. And here the State Department was expressing what seems clearly to have been the predominant mood of the American people, so long mistrustful of European power politics. The Republicans shared the true faith. John Foster Dulles argued that the great threat to peace after the war would lie in the revival of sphere-of-influence thinking. The United States, he said, must not permit Britain and Russia to revert to these bad old ways; it must therefore insist on American participation in all policy decisions for all territories in the world. Dulles wrote pessimistically in January 1945, "The three great powers which at Moscow agreed upon the 'closest cooperation' about European questions have shifted to a practice of separate, regional responsibility."

It is true that critics, and even friends, of the United States sometimes noted a discrepancy between the American passion for universalism when it applied to territory far from American shores and the preeminence the United States accorded its own interests nearer home. Churchill, seeking Washington's blessing for a sphere-of-influence initiative in Eastern Europe, could not forbear reminding the Americans, "We follow the lead of the United States in South America;" nor did any universalist of record propose the abolition of the Monroe Doctrine. But a convenient myopia prevented such inconsistencies from qualifying the ardency of the universalist faith.

There seem only to have been three officials in the United States Government who dissented. One was the Secretary of War, Henry L. Stimson, a classical balance-of-power man, who in 1944 opposed the creation of a vacuum in Central Europe by the pastoralization of Germany and in 1945 urged "the settlement of all territorial acquisitions in the shape of defense posts which each of these four powers may deem to be necessary for their own safety" in advance of any effort to establish a peacetime United Nations. Stimson considered the claim of Russia to a preferred position in Eastern Europe as not unreasonable: as he told President Truman, "he thought the Russians perhaps were being more realistic than we were in regard to their own security." Such a position for Russia seemed to him comparable to the preferred American position in Latin America; he even spoke of "our respective orbits." Stimson was therefore skeptical of what he regarded as the prevailing tendency "to hang on to exaggerated views of the Monroe Doctrine and at the same time butt into every question that comes up in Central Europe." Acceptance of spheres of influence seemed to him the way to avoid "a head-on collision."

A second official opponent of universalism was George Kennan, an eloquent advocate from the American Embassy in Moscow of "a prompt and clear recognition of the division of Europe into spheres of influence and of a policy based on the fact of such division." Kennan argued that nothing we could do would possibly alter the course of events in Eastern Europe; that we were deceiving ourselves by supposing that these countries had any future but Russian domination; that we should therefore relinquish Eastern Europe to the Soviet Union and avoid anything which would make things easier for the Russians by giving them economic assistance or by sharing moral responsibility for their actions.

A third voice within the government against universalism was (at least after the war) Henry A. Wallace. As Secretary of Commerce, he stated the sphere-of-influence case with trenchancy in the famous Madison Square Garden speech of September 1946 which led to his dismissal by President Truman:

On our part, we should recognize that we have no more business in the *political* affairs of Eastern Europe than Russia has in the *political* affairs of Latin America, Western Europe, and the United States. ... Whether we like it or not, the Russians will try to socialize their sphere of influence just as we try to democratize our sphere of influence. ... The Russians have no more business stirring up native Communists to political activity in Western Europe, Latin America, and the United States than we have in interfering with the politics of Eastern Europe and Russia.

Stimson, Kennan and Wallace seem to have been alone in the government, however, in taking these views. They were very much minority voices. Meanwhile universalism, rooted in the American legal and moral tradition, overwhelmingly backed by contemporary opinion, received successive enshrinements in the Atlantic Charter of 1941, in the Declaration of the United Nations in 1942 and in the Moscow Declaration of 1943.

The Kremlin, on the other hand, thought *only* of spheres of interest; above all, the Russians were determined to protect their frontiers, and especially their border to the west, crossed so often and so bloodily in the dark course of their history. These western frontiers lacked natural means of defense—no great oceans, rugged mountains, steaming swamps or impenetrable jungles. The history of Russia had been the history of invasion, the last of which was by now horribly killing up to twenty million of its people. The protocol of Russia therefore meant the enlargement of the area of Russian influence. Kennan himself wrote (in May 1944), "Behind Russia's stubborn expansion lies only the age-old sense of insecurity of a sedentary people reared on an exposed plain in the neighborhood of fierce nomadic peoples," and he called this "urge" a "permanent feature of Russian psychology."

In earlier times the "urge" had produced the tsarist search for buffer states and maritime outlets. In 1939 the Soviet-Nazi pact and its secret protocol had enabled Russia to begin to satisfy in the Baltic states, Karelian Finland and Poland, part of what it conceived as its security requirements in Eastern Europe. But the "urge" persisted, causing the friction between Russia and Germany in 1940 as each jostled for position in the area which separated them. Later it led to Molotov's new demands on Hitler in November 1940—a free hand in Finland, Soviet predominance in Rumania and Bulgaria, bases in the Dardanelles—the demands which convinced Hitler that he had no choice but to attack Russia. Now Stalin hoped to gain from the West what Hitler, a closer neighbor, had not dared yield him.

It is true that, so long as Russian survival appeared to require a second front to relieve the Nazi pressure, Moscow's demand for Eastern Europe was a little muffled. Thus the Soviet government adhered to the Atlantic Charter (though with a significant if obscure reservation about adapting its principles to "the circumstances, needs, and historic peculiarities of particular countries"). Thus it also adhered to the Moscow Declaration of 1943, and Molotov then, with his easy mendacity, even denied that Russia had any desire to divide Europe into spheres of influence. But this was guff, which the Russians were perfectly willing to ladle out if it would keep the Americans, and especially Secretary Hull (who made a strong personal impression at the Moscow conference) happy. "A declaration," as Stalin once observed to Eden, "I regard as algebra, but an agreement as practical arithmetic. I do not wish to decry algebra, but I prefer practical arithmetic."

The more consistent Russian purpose was revealed when Stalin offered the British a straight sphere-of-influence deal at the end of 1941. Britain, he suggested, should recognize the Russian absorption of the Baltic states, part of Finland, eastern Poland and Bessarabia; in return, Russia would support any special British need for bases or security arrangements in Western Europe. There was nothing specifically communist about these ambitions. If Stalin achieved them, he would be fulfilling an age-old dream of the tsars. The British reaction was mixed. "Soviet policy is amoral," as Anthony Eden noted at the time; "United States policy is exaggeratedly moral, at least where non-American interests are concerned." If Roosevelt was a universalist with occasional leanings toward spheres of influence and Stalin was a sphere-of-influence man with occasional gestures toward universalism, Churchill seemed evenly poised between the familiar realism of the balance of power, which he had so long recorded as an historian and manipulated as a statesman, and the hope that there must be some better way of doing things. His 1943 proposal of a world organization divided into regional councils represented an effort to blend universalist and sphere-of-interest conceptions. His initial rejection of Stalin's proposal in December 1941 as "directly contrary to the first, second and third articles of the Atlantic Charter" thus did not spring entirely from a desire to propitiate the United States. On the other hand, he had himself already reinterpreted the Atlantic Charter as applying only to Europe (and thus not to the British Empire), and he was, above all, an empiricist who never believed in sacrificing reality on the altar of doctrine.

So in April 1942 he wrote Roosevelt that "the increasing gravity of the war" had led him to feel that the Charter "ought not to be construed so as to deny Russia the frontiers she occupied when Germany attacked her." Hull, however, remained fiercely hostile to the inclusion of territorial provisions in the Anglo-Russian treaty; the American position, Eden noted, "chilled me with Wilsonian memories." Though Stalin complained that it looked "as if the Atlantic Charter was directed against the U.S.S.R.," it was the Russian season of military adversity in the spring of 1942, and he dropped his demands.

He did not, however, change his intentions. A year later Ambassador Standley could cable Washington from Moscow: "In 1918 Western Europe attempted to set up a *cordon sanitaire* to protect it from the influence of bolshevism. Might not now the Kremlin envisage the formation of a belt of pro-Soviet states to protect it from the influences of the West?" It well might; and that purpose became increasingly clear as the war approached its end. Indeed, it derived sustenance from Western policy in the first area of liberation.

The unconditional surrender of Italy in July 1943 created the first major test of the Western devotion to universalism. America and Britain, having won the Italian war, handled the capitulation, keeping Moscow informed at a distance. Stalin complained:

The United States and Great Britain made agreements but the Soviet Union received information about the results . . . just as a passive third observer. I have to tell you that it is impossible to tolerate the situation any longer. I propose that the [tripartite military-political commission] be established and that Sicily be assigned . . . as its place of residence.

Roosevelt, who had no intention of sharing the control of Italy with the Russians, suavely replied with the suggestion that Stalin send an officer "to General Eisenhower's headquarters in connection with the commission." Unimpressed, Stalin continued to press for a tripartite body;

but his Western allies were adamant in keeping the Soviet Union off the Control Commission for Italy, and the Russians in the end had to be satisfied with a seat, along with minor Allied states, on a meaningless Inter-Allied Advisory Council. Their acquiescence in this was doubtless not unconnected with a desire to establish precedents for Eastern Europe.

Teheran in December 1943 marked the high point of three-power collaboration. Still, when Churchill asked about Russian territorial interests, Stalin replied a little ominously, "There is no need to speak at the present time about any Soviet desires, but when the time comes we will speak." In the next weeks, there were increasing indications of a Soviet determination to deal unilaterally with Eastern Europe—so much so that in early February 1944 Hull cabled Harriman in Moscow:

Matters are rapidly approaching the point where the Soviet Government will have to choose between the development and extension of the foundation of international cooperation as the guiding principle of the postwar world as against the continuance of a unilateral and arbitrary method of dealing with its special problems even though these problems are admittedly of more direct interest to the Soviet Union than to other great powers.

As against this approach, however, Churchill, more tolerant of sphere-of-influence deviations, soon proposed that, with the impending liberation of the Balkans, Russia should run things in Rumania and Britain in Greece. Hull strongly opposed this suggestion but made the mistake of leaving Washington for a few days; and Roosevelt, momentarily free from his Wilsonian conscience, yielded to Churchill's plea for a three-months' trial. Hull resumed the fight on his return, and Churchill postponed the matter.

The Red Army continued its advance into Eastern Europe. In August the Polish

Home Army, urged on by Polish-language broadcasts from Moscow, rose up against the Nazis in Warsaw. For 63 terrible days, the Poles fought valiantly on, while the Red Army halted on the banks of the Vistula a few miles away, and in Moscow Stalin for more than half this time declined to cooperate with the Western effort to drop supplies to the Warsaw Resistance. It appeared a calculated Soviet decision to let the Nazis slaughter the anti-Soviet Polish underground; and, indeed, the result was to destroy any substantial alternative to a Soviet solution in Poland. The agony of Warsaw caused the most deep and genuine moral shock in Britain and America and provoked dark forebodings about Soviet postwar purposes.

Again history enjoins the imaginative leap in order to see things for a moment from Moscow's viewpoint. The Polish question, Churchill would say at Yalta, was for Britain a question of honor. "It is not only a question of honor for Russia," Stalin replied, "but one of life and death. . . . Throughout history Poland had been the corridor for attack on Russia." A top postwar priority for any Russian régime must be to close that corridor. The Home Army was led by anti-communists. It clearly hoped by its action to forestall the Soviet occupation of Warsaw and, in Russian eyes, to prepare the way for an anti-Russian Poland. In addition, the uprising from a strictly operational viewpoint was premature. The Russians, it is evident in retrospect, had real military problems at the Vistula. The Soviet attempt in September to send Polish units from the Red Army across the river to join forces with the Home Army was a disaster. Heavy German shelling thereafter prevented the ferrying of tanks necessary for an assault on the German position. The Red Army itself did not take Warsaw for another three months. None the less, Stalin's indif-

ference to the human tragedy, his effort to blackmail the London Poles during the ordeal, his sanctimonious opposition during five precious weeks to aerial resupply, the invariable coldness of his explanations ("the Soviet command has come to the conclusion that it must dissociate itself from the Warsaw adventure") and the obvious political benefit to the Soviet Union from the destruction of the Home Army— all these had the effect of suddenly dropping the mask of wartime comradeship and displaying to the West the hard face of Soviet policy. In now pursuing what he grimly regarded as the minimal requirements for the postwar security of his country, Stalin was inadvertently showing the irreconcilability of both his means and his ends with the Anglo-American conception of the peace.

Meanwhile Eastern Europe presented the Alliance with still another crisis that same September. Bulgaria, which was not at war with Russia, decided to surrender to the Western Allies while it still could; and the English and Americans at Cairo began to discuss armistice terms with Bulgarian envoys. Moscow, challenged by what it plainly saw as a Western intrusion into its own zone of vital interest, promptly declared war on Bulgaria, took over the surrender negotiations and, invoking the Italian precedent, denied its Western Allies any role in the Bulgarian Control Commission. In a long and thoughtful cable, Ambassador Harriman meditated on the problems of communication with the Soviet Union. "Words," he reflected, "have a different connotation to the Soviets than they have to us. When they speak of insisting on 'friendly governments' in their neighboring countries, they have in mind something quite different from what we would mean." The Russians, he surmised, really believed that Washington accepted "their position that although they would keep us informed they had the right to settle their problems with their western neighbors unilaterally." But the Soviet position was still in flux: "the Soviet Government is not one mind." The problem, as Harriman had earlier told Harry Hopkins, was "to strengthen the hands of those around Stalin who want to play the game along our lines." The way to do this, he now told Hull, was to

be understanding of their sensitivity, meet them much more than half way, encourage them and support them wherever we can, and yet oppose them promptly with the greatest of firmness where we see them going wrong. . . . The only way we can eventually come to an understanding with the Soviet Union on the question of non-interference in the internal affairs of other countries is for us to take a definite interest in the solution of the problems of each individual country as they arise.

As against Harriman's sophisticated universalist strategy, however, Churchill, increasingly fearful of the consequences of unrestrained competition in Eastern Europe, decided in early October to carry his sphere-of-influence proposal directly to Moscow. Roosevelt was at first content to have Churchill speak for him too and even prepared a cable to that effect. But Hopkins, a more rigorous universalist, took it upon himself to stop the cable and warn Roosevelt of its possible implications. Eventually Roosevelt sent a message to Harriman in Moscow emphasizing that he expected to "retain complete freedom of action after this conference is over." It was now that Churchill quickly proposed—and Stalin as quickly accepted—the celebrated division of southeastern Europe: ending (after further haggling between Eden and Molotov) with 90 percent Soviet predominance in Rumania, 80 percent in Bulgaria and Hungary, fifty-fifty in Jugoslavia, 90 percent British predominance in Greece. Churchill in discussing this with Harriman used the phrase "spheres of influ-

ence." But he insisted that these were only "immediate wartime arrangements" and received a highly general blessing from Roosevelt. Yet, whatever Churchill intended, there is reason to believe that Stalin construed the percentages as an agreement, not a declaration; as practical arithmetic, not algebra. For Stalin, it should be understood, the sphere-of-influence idea did not mean that he would abandon all efforts to spread communism in some other nation's sphere; it did mean that, if he tried this and the other side cracked down, he could not feel he had serious cause for complaint. As Kennan wrote to Harriman at the end of 1944:

As far as border states are concerned the Soviet government has never ceased to think in terms of spheres of interest. They expect us to support them in whatever action they wish to take in those regions, regardless of whether that action seems to us or to the rest of the world to be right or wrong. . . . I have no doubt that this position is honestly maintained on their part, and that they would be equally prepared to reserve moral judgment on any actions which we might wish to carry out, i.e., in the Caribbean area.

In any case, the matter was already under test a good deal closer to Moscow than the Caribbean. The communist-dominated resistance movement in Greece was in open revolt against the effort of the Papandreou government to disarm and disband the guerrillas (the same Papandreou whom the Greek colonels have recently arrested on the claim that he is a tool of the communists). Churchill now called in British Army units to crush the insurrection. This action produced a storm of criticism in his own country and in the United States; the American Government even publicly dissociated itself from the intervention, thereby emphasizing its detachment from the sphere-of-influence deal. But Stalin, Churchill later claimed, "adhered strictly and faithfully to our agreement of October, and during all the long weeks of fighting the Communists in the streets of Athens not one word of reproach came from *Pravda* or *Izvestia*," though there is no evidence that he tried to call off the Greek communists. Still, when the communist rebellion later broke out again in Greece, Stalin told Kardelj and Djilas of Jugoslavia in 1948, "The uprising in Greece must be stopped, and as quickly as possible."

No one, of course, can know what really was in the minds of the Russian leaders. The Kremlin archives are locked; of the primary actors, only Molotov survives, and he has not yet indicated any desire to collaborate with the Columbia Oral History Project. We do know that Stalin did not wholly surrender to sentimental illusion about his new friends. In June 1944, on the night before the landings in Normandy, he told Djilas that the English "find nothing sweeter than to trick their allies. . . . And Churchill? Churchill is the kind who, if you don't watch him, will slip a kopeck out of your pocket. Yes, a kopeck out of your pocket! . . . Roosevelt is not like that. He dips in his hand only for bigger coins." But whatever his views of his colleagues it is not unreasonable to suppose that Stalin would have been satisfied at the end of the war to secure what Kennan has called "a protective glacis along Russia's western border," and that, in exchange for a free hand in Eastern Europe, he was prepared to give the British and Americans equally free hands in their zones of vital interest, including in nations as close to Russia as Greece (for the British) and, very probably—or at least so the Jugoslavs believe—China (for the United States). In other words, his initial objectives were very probably not world conquest but Russian security.

It is now pertinent to inquire why the United States rejected the idea of stabilizing the world by division into spheres of influence and insisted on an East European strategy. One should warn against rushing to the conclusion that it was all a row between hard-nosed, balance-of-power realists and starry-eyed Wilsonians. Roosevelt, Hopkins, Welles, Harriman, Bohlen, Berle, Dulles and other universalists were tough and serious men. Why then did they rebuff the sphere-of-influence solution?

The first reason is that they regarded this solution as containing within itself the seeds of a third world war. The balance-of-power idea seemed inherently unstable. It had always broken down in the past. It held out to each power the permanent temptation to try to alter the balance in its own favor, and it built this temptation into the international order. It would turn the great powers of 1945 away from the objective of concerting common policies toward competition for postwar advantage. As Hopkins told Molotov at Teheran, "The President feels it essential to world peace that Russia, Great Britain and the United States work out this control question in a manner which will not start each of the three powers arming against the others." "The greatest likelihood of eventual conflict," said the Joint Chiefs of Staff in 1944 (the only conflict which the J.C.S., in its wisdom, could then glimpse "in the foreseeable future" was between Britain and Russia), ". . . would seem to grow out of either nation initiating attempts to build up its strength, by seeking to attach to herself parts of Europe to the disadvantage and possible danger of her potential adversary." The Americans were perfectly ready to acknowledge that Russia was entitled to convincing assurance of her national security—but not this way. "I could sympathize fully with Stalin's desire to protect his western borders from future attack," as Hull put it. "But I felt that this security could best be obtained through a strong postwar peace organization."

Hull's remark suggests the second objection: that the sphere-of-influence approach would, in the words of the State Department in 1945, "militate against the establishment and effective functioning of a broader system of general security in which all countries will have their part." The United Nations, in short, was seen as the alternative to the balance of power. Nor did the universalists see any necessary incompatibility between the Russian desire for "friendly governments" on its frontier and the American desire for self-determination in Eastern Europe. Before Yalta the State Department judged the general mood of Europe as "to the left and strongly in favor of far-reaching economic and social reforms, but not, however, in favor of a left-wing totalitarian regime to achieve these reforms." Governments in Eastern Europe could be sufficiently to the left "to allay Soviet suspicions" but sufficiently representative "of the center and *petit bourgeois* elements" not to seem a prelude to communist dictatorship. The American criteria were therefore that the government "should be dedicated to the preservation of civil liberties" and "should favor social and economic reforms." A string of New Deal states—of Finlands and Czechoslovakias—seemed a reasonable compromise solution.

Third, the universalists feared that the sphere-of-interest approach would be what Hull termed "a haven for the isolationists," who would advocate America's participation in Western Hemisphere affairs on condition that it did not participate in European or Asian affairs. Hull also feared that spheres of interest would lead to "closed trade areas or discriminatory systems" and thus defeat his cherished dream of a low-tariff, freely trading world.

Fourth, the sphere-of-interest solution meant the betrayal of the principles for which the Second World War was being fought—the Atlantic Charter, the Four Freedoms, the Declaration of the United Nations. Poland summed up the problem. Britain, having gone to war to defend the independence of Poland from the Germans, could not easily conclude the war by surrendering the independence of Poland to the Russians. Thus, as Hopkins told Stalin after Roosevelt's death in 1945, Poland had "become the symbol of our ability to work out problems with the Soviet Union." Nor could American liberals in general watch with equanimity while the police state spread into countries which, if they had mostly not been real democracies, had mostly not been tyrannies either. The execution in 1943 of Ehrlich and Alter, the Polish socialist trade union leaders, excited deep concern. "I have particularly in mind," Harriman cabled in 1944, "objection to the institution of secret police who may become involved in the persecution of persons of truly democratic convictions who may not be willing to conform to Soviet methods."

Fifth, the sphere-of-influence solution would create difficult domestic problems in American politics. Roosevelt was aware of the six million or more Polish votes in the 1944 election; even more acutely, he was aware of the broader and deeper attack which would follow if, after going to war to stop the Nazi conquest of Europe, he permitted the war to end with the communist conquest of Eastern Europe. As Archibald MacLeish, then Assistant Secretary of State for Public Affairs, warned in January 1945, "The wave of disillusionment which has distressed us in the last several weeks will be increased if the impression is permitted to get abroad that potentially totalitarian provisional governments are to be set up without adequate safeguards as to the holding of free elections and the realization of the principles of the Atlantic Charter." Roosevelt believed that no administration could survive which did not try everything short of war to save Eastern Europe, and he was the supreme American politician of the century.

Sixth, if the Russians were allowed to overrun Eastern Europe without argument, would that satisfy them? Even Kennan, in a dispatch of May 1944, admitted that the "urge" had dreadful potentialities: "If initially successful, will it know where to stop? Will it not be inexorably carried forward, by its very nature, in a struggle to reach the whole—to attain complete mastery of the shores of the Atlantic and the Pacific?" His own answer was that there were inherent limits to the Russian capacity to expand—"that Russia will not have an easy time in maintaining the power which it has seized over other people in Eastern and Central Europe unless it receives both moral and material assistance from the West." Subsequent developments have vindicated Kennan's argument. By the late forties, Jugoslavia and Albania, the two East European states farthest from the Soviet Union and the two in which communism was imposed from within rather than from without, had declared their independence of Moscow. But, given Russia's success in maintaining centralized control over the international communist movement for a quarter of a century, who in 1944 could have had much confidence in the idea of communist revolts against Moscow?

Most of those involved therefore rejected Kennan's answer and stayed with his question. If the West turned its back on East-ern Europe, the higher probability, in their view, was that the Russians would use their security zone, not just for defensive purposes, but as a springboard from which to mount an attack on Western Europe, now shattered by war, a vacuum of power awaiting its master. "If the policy is accepted that the Soviet Union has a right to penetrate her immediate neighbors for security," Harriman said in 1944, "penetration of the next immediate neighbors becomes at a certain time equally logical." If a row with Russia were inevitable, every consideration of prudence dictated that it should take place in Eastern rather than Western Europe.

Thus idealism and realism joined in opposition to the sphere-of-influence solution. The consequence was a determination to assert an American interest in the postwar destiny of all nations, including those of Eastern Europe. In the message which Roosevelt and Hopkins drafted after Hopkins had stopped Roosevelt's initial cable authorizing Churchill to speak for the United States at the Moscow meeting of October 1944, Roosevelt now said, "There is in this global war literally no question, either military or political, in which the United States is not interested." After Roosevelt's death Hopkins repeated the point to Stalin: "The cardinal basis of President Roosevelt's policy which the American people had fully supported had been the concept that the interests of the U.S. were worldwide and not confined to North and South America and the Pacific Ocean."

The American policy of unconditional surrender has been criticized for prolonging the war, undermining German resistance to Hitler's regime, and opening a power vacuum in Central and Eastern Europe to Russian control. One advocate of this interpretation is ANNE ARMSTRONG (b. 1924), an assistant professor of political science at Hunter College, The City University of New York, and the author of *Unconditional Surrender: The Impact of the Casablanca Policy upon World War II* (1961). Does Armstrong make an effective case against the effects of the unconditional surrender policy? And does she suggest a realistic alternative to that strategy?*

Anne Armstrong

Shortsighted and Destructive

The Casablanca Formula of Unconditional Surrender is symptomatic of an attitude toward war which tends to divide strategy from political goals. In the Second World War American long-range political objectives played a secondary role. In the major conferences of the war, at least until the last year, strategy took precedence over diplomacy. Decisions of the greatest political importance were made primarily, even solely, on the basis of military considerations, as, for example, the routes the invading Allied armies would follow or which ally would take Berlin. It is true that the American planners were dedicated to a final goal in the war, but they perceived that goal as simply total victory, the total destruction of the military power of the Axis enemy.

There appear to have been at least three roots of this "win the war first" mentality: military, political, and ideological. In retrospect it may be difficult to take the military basis seriously, to grant that sheer military necessity dictated the attention first to strategic planning. In retrospect it is difficult to recapture the tensions and fears of 1943 but certainly, to some degree at least, the focusing of Allied planning on immediate military problems, on the marshaling of troops, the sinking of submarines, and the achievement of air superiority rather than on diplomatic objectives was due to the psychology engendered by the dazzling

*From Anne Armstrong, *Unconditional Surrender: The Impact of the Casablanca Policy upon World War II* (New Brunswick, N.J.: Rutgers University Press, 1961), pp. 249–262. Footnotes omitted.

German victories in the war's early years, to the blitzkrieg in the West, and the rapid advance of the Wehrmacht to the gates of Moscow and Leningrad and Stalingrad. The argument that military victory which does not secure the political conditions essential for peace or for the preservation of national safety and interest is not strategic victory is not answered by a reference to the psychology of 1943, but such an explanation can, at least, make the error intelligible.

The political roots of the doctrine of winning the war first were complex and serious. The Western fear that the U.S.S.R. might withdraw from the alliance by arranging a separate peace with Germany was apparently not entirely groundless. Whether or not the Soviets intended to negotiate with the Nazi government they did not hesitate to use the threat that they might do so as a weapon in winning concessions from the West. It was certainly in the Western interest to keep the U.S.S.R. in the war. Critics of the concessions made will probably quarrel with the degree and the method of bargaining rather than with the aim.

Even within the Anglo-American alliance there was some degree of suspicion and division. The Americans, on the one hand, seemed to fear that British interest in the Mediterranean and the Balkans represented narrow British nationalism, imperial interests, and power politics, and therefore they often opposed British proposals to side with the Soviet Union. The English, on the other hand, were often forced to regard their American partners as naïve and shortsighted, guided more by enthusiasm than by experience and sagacity. However, within the American camp itself there was division: General Wedemeyer, for example, opposed the doctrine of Unconditional Surrender and General Clark favored the British plan for a Balkan invasion route; Secretaries Hull and Stimson differed sharply with Morgenthau on plans for [the deindustrialization of] Germany. Within the American Senate isolationism was by no means dead, Roosevelt's postwar plans were never sure of unquestioning acceptance.

The ideological root of a doctrine of total defeat of the enemy, that is, in the doctrine of moral war, seems to lie in the nature of modern democracy. Modern war requires mass participation in the armed service, in industry, and in war work. In a democracy, and probably also in a dictatorship, this requires the moral support of the general public for the war. One of the ways in which such popular support can be secured is by making the war a clear-cut moral issue, by asserting that it is being fought to right a wrong, by branding the enemy as totally guilty, as criminals, aggressors, and militarists. Throughout the war stories of the enemy's atrocities are used to increase public willingness to make sacrifices. Popular emotions of fear and hatred are evoked, and these emotions once evoked become in themselves a political force which may make rational political decisions unpopular or even impossible. In the instance of the Second World War the propaganda offensive seems to have been so successful that even the makers of policy themselves seem to have accepted the tenets of propaganda as the bases for policy. The dogma that Prussia-Germany was the perpetual aggressor in European warfare, the official view of the exaggerated political importance of the German General Staff, the theory of the dangers to democracy, lawful government, and peace inherent in Prussia and especially in its ruling class, the doctrine of the conspiracy of the industrialists, Junkers, and militarists to push Hitler into power, a dogma that was at least open to question and critical historical analysis, seems never to have been criticized in official circles during the war, at least not in the recorded public discussions of memoranda or memoirs. The dissension from Morgenthauism was made on grounds of impracticality; it was criticized as an ineffective means not as an end.

The basic assumptions of Roosevelt's aims in Germany—the assumptions that Germany alone had been primarily responsible for all recent international war and tension, that peace could be established by destroying the roots of aggression in Germany—seem never to have been questioned. There were arguments over the degree of control, the extent of dismantling, the exact nature of the Nürnberg trials but never, publicly, over the view of history and of warfare on which these plans were based. There was no open questioning of the total guilt of the enemy, no questioning of the moral right of the United States to bring what would amount to a social, legal, and economic revolution to the center of Europe. This was the unchallenged right of the victor, of the innocent nation. Within the framework of this attitude, which can be described as Calvinistic or naïve, there was no alternative to the war aim of total defeat of the enemy.

Since the war is viewed as a massive struggle of the forces of good against the forces of evil, no compromise is thinkable. Compromise is possible only between human beings who recognize each other as human, as mutually fallible, not between abstract forces, and most certainly not between abstract Good and Evil.

Such a categorical view renders flexibility of policy almost impossible. Not only is compromise with the Nazi government in Germany unthinkable, but also compromise with any group or faction within Germany, certainly a group centered around Junkers and militarists. The very existence of an anti-Nazi group within Germany became a cause of embarrassment for the Roosevelt administration. Compromise concerning the ends of war policy rather than merely the details of the means became impossible.

Throughout the war there were suggestions by American generals, American Cabinet officials, the Soviet and British governments that the Casablanca Formula be abandoned or modified or at least explained. These were not demands for the alteration of the basic aim of the war; that would remain the total defeat of the enemy. These demands were for the modification of the phrase "Unconditional Surrender" as a propaganda slogan. Consistently the President rejected all demands for the abandonment or modification of Unconditional Surrender, repeating again and again the anecdote about Lee and Grant at Appomattox. Although the presidential version of the historical origin of Unconditional Surrender was inaccurate, it revealed a symbolic truth: the President thought of the Second World War as at least analogous to the American Civil War. Traditionally diplomacy has distinguished sharply between civil wars—which are essentially rebellions in which the rebels have acted in violation of established order, have committed a criminal act by the resort to violence, and in which there can be no compromise—and a war between two or more sovereign states. The President seems not to have made this traditional distinction. For him the Second World War was a species of civil war, a war of the forces of law against the forces of totalitarianism and aggression. That the struggle was being waged in coalition with a power that had been a full partner in the aggression of 1939 and that was at least as totalitarian as Nazi Germany seems not to have disturbed the logic of Unconditional

Surrender. The policy and the demand remained.

The demand was fulfilled in May, 1945. The total power of Germany had been destroyed. The victorious armies of the four powers marched through the streets of Berlin. The four powers assumed supreme authority in Germany. Total victory had been achieved.

What had been its costs? Was the achievement worth the cost? Had there been a practicable alternative which might have produced more favorable results? It is impossible to answer these questions with any degree of accuracy. Even the specific military question of whether the demand for unconditional surrender lengthened and intensified the war cannot be answered absolutely. If the phrase "Unconditional Surrender" is interpreted as the policy of refusal to compromise, of rejecting a negotiated solution, then it seems quite clear that it did lengthen the war, or at least that the leaders of the German Wehrmacht, had they been in a position to make their decisions effective, would have been willing to negotiate on the basis of compromise much earlier than May, 1945. Three German field marshals have recorded their opinions that Germany had lost all chance of achieving strategic victory in the war after the Stalingrad disaster, that they would have considered a compromise solution at that time intelligent. After the defeat of the German and Italian forces in North Africa, in spring, 1943, Rommel concluded unequivocally that the German cause was hopeless. By July, 1944, when the Allies broke through the German encirclement of their Normandy beach-head and secured the open plain leading to Paris and Germany, dozens of German generals on both the Eastern and the Western Front concluded that total eventual defeat of the Wehrmacht had become inevitable. In the East the Red Army was driving toward the German border, the Crimea had been lost, the Soviets had penetrated into Rumania. Keitel confessed: "Even I know that there is no more to be done." On July 15 Rommel prepared a memorandum for Hitler urging him to accept the political consequences of the military situation. Hitler refused.

No one succeeded in estimating the political consequences of the military situation. Germany had lost the war, but the fighting continued for nine months longer. The impressive list of German generals who insist that Germany could not have secured victory after Stalingrad, January, 1943, and conclude that Germany had decisively lost the war by July, 1944, state that they, as commanders, would have been willing to participate in and agree to negotiations for a compromise settlement, but rather than submit to Unconditional Surrender they and their troops continued the hopeless struggle until May, 1945. It seems clear that had the German generals been able to act to end the war and had the Allies been willing to negotiate, the war might have ended earlier, nine months to two years earlier depending on the degree of compromise.

The exact nature of the peace that might have ensued at an earlier date than that of Germany's unconditional surrender cannot be accurately constructed in retrospect. Since it would have been a solution arrived at by the process of bargaining, based on mutual compromise, it is difficult to know what details of final settlement might ultimately have been accepted. However, the generals interviewed were in substantial agreement that in July, 1944, they would have been willing to accept in principle the payment of reparations for war damages, the surrender of all territory gained by conquest, disarmament, and the trial of alleged war criminals under accepted principles of existent international law. A compromise solution could very likely not have included the unconditional surrender aims of four-power military occupation of the German Reich, and of Allied assumption of full power to pursue the policy of denazification, demilitarization, and punishment of war criminals. The compromise solution would very likely have been a treaty with the West alone.

It is also impossible to prove the exact degree of effect the Allied Unconditional Surrender policy had on the German anti-Nazi resistance movement, but it is clear that the leaders of this movement were in agreement that the effect was negative. The anti-Nazis could hope to succeed in overthrowing Hitler and the SS and Gestapo only if they could secure the active co-operation of sufficient troop commanders to throw the balance of military strength for and not against a possible coup d'état. Although they did succeed in winning the support of many military leaders [in July 1944], many crucial commanders withheld active support. Kesselring, although not approached in regard to the plan, writes that he would not have participated as long as the alternative to Hitler remained unconditional surrender. Manstein agreed, and both Guderian and Jodl gave as explicit reasons for their refusal to co-operate with the plot the alternative of unconditional surrender. Even Field Marshal von Witzleben, an original member of the conspiracy, was shaken by the final refusal of the Allies to compromise or to negotiate. He felt that no honorable man could overthrow the government in the face of the demand for unconditional surrender and was ready to withdraw support from the plot, but he was convinced by Schlabrendorff's argument that by then the stakes were no longer German existence, but German honor.

The choice was not a simple one. Many key commanders refused to join the conspiracy. Despite this, *Operation Walküre* was launched and ran its tragic course. It cannot be proved with historical accuracy that the participation of a few more military commanders would have ensured the victory of the plot nor that the commanders who refused co-operation on ground of unconditional surrender would actually have brought themselves to act had an alternative policy been extant; however, there is room to speculate that some truth might lie in the twin deductions. In any event, the uncompromising demand for unconditional surrender was at least a factor in the failure of the plot and certainly did not strengthen the hand of the resistance leaders.

Had the plot succeeded, had the anti-Nazi leaders succeeded in their plan to assume control in Germany, arrest the Gestapo and SS leadership, and intern the heads of the Nazi government, they certainly intended to sue for peace. Their plans included the re-establishment of constitutional government in Germany, the denazification of the government and public life, and the trial under established law of alleged war criminals. The new provisional government would have sought a peace which would guarantee German sovereignty and unity on the basis of the prewar boundaries. Whether such a solution would have been more in the interests of the United States and of the West is a question that can be more dispassionately answered now, perhaps, than would have been possible in 1945. The failure to achieve such a solution, the failure of the 1944 plot, was costly to Germany if not to the West. The loss of leadership involved in the execution of men like Beck, Goerdeler, Stauffenberg, Witzleben, Trott, Moltke, Leuschner, and hundreds more has been felt in postwar Germany. The failure to end the war in 1944 brought about the death and torture of thousands of Germans and non-Germans in Gestapo prisons and concentration camps month by month until the final end in May, 1945.

The cost of the failure of the plot and the costs of the continuation of the war cannot be attributed solely to the Casablanca Formula, but surely the facts seem to warrant the conclusion that had the Allies been in a frame of mind to seek a solution there were Germans who would have been eager to meet them at least halfway.

The proposition that a policy other than the demand for the total defeat of Germany might have resulted in the saving of lives, the sparing of cities from complete devastation, the preservation of valuable human and cultural and economic resources important to all Europe and to the West, as well as to Germany, depends for its validity on the assumption that an alternative policy would have served better the interests of the United States and of the West and on the further assumption that such an alternative would have been practicable.

The acceptance by the United States of an alternate policy to Unconditional Surrender would have necessitated a basically different view from that of war as the punishment of the guilty by the innocent. Had the American planners accepted the traditional view of Clausewitz—that military operations in war are the servants of policy, that the goal of all war is to achieve a political objective by one means or another, and that the defeat of the enemy on the field of battle is only one such means— there might have been less tendency to rivet attention on the means rather than on the ends. If the dominant question of the policy makers had been "What ends would best serve American interests?" the answer

might have been not the punishment of aggression, the destruction of the enemy, but rather the prevention or at least the discouragement of future war and the establishment in Europe of conditions which would tend to foster peace.

What were the basic American and Western interests in Europe? Perhaps, in general terms, these: (1) the creation of conditions less likely than those of the 1930's to precipitate war and international crisis; (2) the abolition of totalitarianism in Germany; (3) the establishment of a system in Europe which would add to the security and independence of smaller states; (4) a relatively prosperous and stable European economy as a prerequisite to political stability and freedom; (5) the furtherance of the principles of international law and of civilized intercourse among states.

Surely aims not greatly different from these seem to have underlain the American wartime plans for the occupation of Germany, for denazification, and for the Nürnberg trials. Such aims are realistic and moral. How successful were the means? Did the policy of Unconditional Surrender and the implementation that it implied lead to stability and peace or to chaos and to the Cold War?

The conclusions of those closely associated with denazification, for example, indicate that the zealous American attempts to revamp German society in the postwar era proved costly and far from overwhelmingly successful. The Nürnberg trials have provoked serious criticism by jurists of many nations and now form the precedent for Soviet charges that the West is currently engaging in a conspiracy to wage aggressive warfare against the Communist nations. The four-power occupation that had been designed to bring democracy to Germany and peace to Europe has brought Communism to East Germany and a hostile division between East and West to the world. The small nations of Eastern Europe have been rescued from the theories of [the Nazi philosopher, Alfred] Rosenberg only to be delivered over to the theories of Lenin and the practice of Stalin. The war, begun to secure the independence of Poland and Czechoslovakia, ended with Soviet domination of Eastern and Central Europe.

Could there have been an alternative policy which would more nearly have fulfilled the original aims of American planners? Many writers assert that there could have been. As early as 1943 the English military analyst Basil Liddell Hart urged his government to consider the future balance of Europe, warning that the preponderance of Russian power in postwar Europe would pose a menace to British interests. He contended that the predominance of any one nation in Europe has always tended to precipitate wars: "Acton's famous dictum that 'absolute power corrupts absolutely' applies to nations as well as to individual rulers." He pointed out the growing emphasis on military power in the Soviet system as demonstrated, for example, in the increased attention given to military training under the revised Soviet educational system, and he concluded that postwar Soviet imperialistic expansion might be the ultimate result. By 1943 it was clear that Russia intended to absorb the Baltic States and a large part of Poland, and he warned that the "process of extending frontiers for greater security easily develops a habit of further extensions for greater power—as history reminds us." Victory in Europe would be in a large measure due to the efforts of the Red Army, or at least the U.S.S.R. would believe so, and would result in Soviet occupation of the whole of Central Europe and a large part of Germany. Liddell Hart was

afraid that a political crisis in Western and Southern Europe might result because the parties of the left in those areas would gravitate to the Soviet sphere of influence and might appeal to the Soviet government for aid in struggles with their own governments. He concluded that unfortunately the only state which could provide a stable element in Europe and could effectively serve as a buffer against Soviet expansion was "the one we are now aiming to smash." He concluded that German aggressive power had been broken:

. . . It was curbed before the winter of 1941, and crippled before the winter of 1942. Indeed, it was a plant that had shallow roots even when it looked most impressive, and could only flourish when nourished by easy success—as was pointed out in successive estimates of the situation that I wrote both before the war and in the autumn of 1939. Its shallowness was clearly shown by the lack of enthusiasm among the mass of the German people at the time their army had its most striking run of success; many neutral observers in Germany have borne witness in 1940–41 to the prevalence of this underlying depression.

While Germany's offensive power has long since waned and could only be revived by blunders on our part, her resources still suffice to provide a large measure of defence power. It is sustained by fear of the consequences of unconditional surrender. . . . The underlying paradox of the situation today is that this defensive power which we are trying to break, and which still presents a formidable obstacle athwart our "path to victory," is at the same time the only Continental element that has sufficient strength to form a stable buttress in Western Europe.

He concluded that the "natural effect of destroying the German Army will be to establish the overwhelming military predominance of the Red Army."

The British generally seem to have taken the view that the aim of the war was to prevent any single power from achieving a position of predominance on the Continent. To prevent Soviet hegemony in Central Europe, Churchill urged Western penetration of the Balkans and Anglo-American capture of Berlin, but such arguments were regarded with suspicion in Washington, at least by President Roosevelt. Roosevelt constantly warned that all anti-Soviet propaganda emanated from the pen of Goebbels and at least some of his official associates shared this view. Eisenhower reportedly feared that the Anglo-Americans might be seduced by the German warnings of Soviet intentions, and in May, 1945, Ambassador Joseph E. Davies confided to [Roosevelt's Chief of Staff,] Admiral Leahy his concern over Churchill's "vehement and violent criticisms" of the Soviet Union:

...I said that frankly, as I had listened to him inveigh so violently against the threat of Soviet domination and the spread of Communism in Europe, and disclose such a lack of confidence in the professions of good faith of Soviet leadership, I had wondered whether he, the Prime Minister, was now willing to declare to the world that he and Great Britain had made a mistake in not supporting Hitler, for as I understood him, he was now expressing the doctrine which Hitler and Goebbels had been proclaiming and reiterating for the past four years in an effort to break up allied unity and "divide and conquer" . . . I simply could not bring myself to believe that his considered judgment or expressions would ultimately confirm such an interpretation.

Ultimately the official view of the American government came to accept and to share the British Prime Minister's fears, but during the Second World War the view of Roosevelt and of his close advisers was that the war must be fought in close cooperation with both major allies, Great Britain and the Soviet Union, and that it was somehow lacking in good faith to express skepticism regarding the political intentions of an ally. There were surely ex-

perts in both the Department of State and the army who prepared memoranda based on a realistic appraisal of Soviet intentions, but these did not affect policy. Sumner Welles, war-time Undersecretary of State, later complained that State Department plans to prevent the worst dangers of the Russian domination of Europe were never implemented and that frequently American policy makers had been outmaneuvered by the Soviets simply because they did not know sufficient history.

Secretary [of Defense] Forrestal also decried his government's lack of realism in planning policy: "The great mistakes were made during the war because of American failure to realize that military and political action had to go hand in hand. Both the British and the Russians realize this fact." He concluded that the Churchill plan to invade Europe by way of the Balkans might have proved militarily costly, "but it would have prevented the Russian domination of the Balkans." Forrestal's over-all conclusion on American wartime policy was that diplomatic planning had been "far below the quality of planning that went into the conduct of the war" and that "comparatively little thought" had been given to the political conditions that would emerge from the destruction of Germany and Japan. He wrote that "the ominous developments in Europe could have left no thoughtful person too happy with the results of 'unconditional surrender.' "

Undoubtedly thought had been given to political objectives and to the realities of history, but the thinking had been done by experts whose views were simply not consulted. There seem to have been two major reasons why no alternative to Unconditional Surrender was even openly discussed during the Second World War: first, that the major decisions regarding aims of policy were made by the President and by his personal advisers as more or less an afterthought to strategic decisions and, second, because the emotions and enthusiasms engendered by the war seem to have blurred the realism of the planners' analysis of German and of Russian history. The statements of President Eisenhower in 1952 sound nothing like the statements of General Eisenhower in 1944 and 1945. The reactions of [President] Truman and [Secretary of State] Byrnes to the fait accompli they encountered at Potsdam were realistic and relatively quick. The revolution in the official American view of both Germany and Russia which began slowly in 1945 and 1946 has gathered momentum. The shock of the Cold War has engendered a realism which could not thrive in the heat of the Second World War. This American *renversement diplomatique* has, in a sense, been a repudiation of both the theory and the content of Unconditional Surrender. It has been an acknowledgment de facto of the realities of the balance of power, and an implicit acknowledgment that perhaps the moral basis of the doctrine of total victory was neither historically nor philosophically sound.

The acceptance of an alternative to the policy of Unconditional Surrender during the Second World War would have demanded a more flexible and a more realistic attitude toward both Germany and Russia, a view of war as the instrument of policy rather than of policy as the hand-maiden of strategy, an attitude toward both war and policy less sentimental, less categorical, and less emotional, a policy designed to achieve ends and not one which became entangled with means. The words "Unconditional Surrender" and the specific aims those words convey, the rejection of compromise, the total defeat of the enemy, total occupation, punishment and re-education of the enemy nation, and total reorganization of enemy society, the pursuit of war to its ultimate conclusion—all this indicates a kind of thinking, an attitude toward war, inimical to a policy of alternatives. The words and the policy Unconditional Surrender reveal the wartime atmosphere of idealism, of enthusiasm, and of hatred, an atmosphere open to criticism on two serious grounds.

It was the realist Bismarck who warned that in politics emotions make a good servant but a bad master. During the Second World War it was a different realist, Pope Pius XII, who in June, 1944, warned President Roosevelt through his envoy, Myron Taylor, that the temple of peace would stand and endure only if established on the foundation of Christian charity, not alloyed with vindictive passion or any elements of hatred. The Pope explained to Taylor that he considered the demand for unconditional surrender incompatible with Christian doctrine.

JOHN L. SNELL (b. 1923), a specialist in German history and the diplomacy of World War II, has written about the *Wartime Origins of the East-West Dilemma Over Germany* (1959) and *The Meaning of Yalta* (1956). In the first of these books, he discusses the formulation and usefulness of the unconditional surrender policy. Does the fact that Armstrong focuses her attention on German views of the policy and that Snell analyzes it from the perspective of American and British interests help explain why they arrive at such different conclusions?*

John L. Snell

Considered and Useful

In January, 1943, . . . Roosevelt publicly announced at Casablanca that the Allies would demand the "unconditional surrender" of the Axis Powers. Actually, Hitler had left them little choice in this, since he had repeatedly proclaimed that Germany faced either total victory or total defeat. "There is to be no capitulation to the powers outside, no revolution by the forces within," he announced on many occasions. Hitler remembered the revolution of 1918. So did Roosevelt and Churchill, who also recalled the Fourteen Points and the way Germany had abused Woodrow Wilson's memory after 1918. Both were determined that there should be no opportunity after World War II for Germans to shout that wartime promises had been broken; there

would be no promises this time. As early as June, 1941, both Roosevelt and Churchill had concluded that there should be no negotiated peace with Hitler. The Casablanca announcement merely made this conclusion public.

The best case that can possibly be made against the unconditional surrender policy has been made by many authors. The case in its favor has seldom been presented. Entries on both sides of the ledger must be considered.

Critics have suggested that Roosevelt made the announcement without consulting his advisers. But the President was informally advised before the Casablanca meeting that a special State Department sub-committee on postwar security prob-

*From John L. Snell, *Wartime Origins of the East-West Dilemma Over Germany* (New Orleans, La.: J. G. Hauser, Inc., 1959), pp. 15–18. Footnotes omitted.

lems thought this policy preferable to a negotiated peace; and the Joint Chiefs of Staff approved the policy in advance of the Casablanca meeting. Critics have insisted that Roosevelt surprised a hapless Churchill with the slogan when he announced it publicly, leaving the Prime Minister little choice but to say: "Me too." In actuality Churchill knew of Roosevelt's intentions five days in advance and even informed the War Cabinet in London of the proposed move. Critics at the time and later argued that it hampered the work of Allied propagandists because it strengthened the internal unity of the German people; but Churchill insisted that any more specific statement of genuine Allied war aims would unite the Germans far more resolutely than would the controversial formula. Critics have insisted that it stiffened the resistance of German troops and it probably did. But an entire German army surrendered at Stalingrad exactly one week after the announcement was made to the world.

Critics have insisted that the slogan discouraged the rise of opposition against Nazism within Germany, and it probably did. But the critics overlook two facts: (1) there was only an inconsequential Resistance movement in Germany before January, 1943; and (2) the Resistance movement grew during the next year-and-a-half and produced two major attempts to assassinate Hitler in 1943–1944. Still other critics insist that Roosevelt's announcement was either a naive or a traitorous device to please the U.S.S.R. But the controversial formula must have been poor consolation to Russians who knew that they would

have to fight on without help on a second front. Stalin privately made known his opposition to the formula soon after it was announced. Pacifists have condemned the formula as a vicious war aim; but other pacifists have seen in it an effort to postpone the task of making peace until the passions of war had cooled.

The most important reason for the formula was that the Allies could discuss specific terms of the future peace settlement only at the risk of disrupting the wartime unity of the three Great Powers. It thus became deliberate American policy in 1942 to adopt no specific policy toward the defeated enemy until after the war. Hull, Roosevelt and the Joint Chiefs of Staff approved this "policy of postponement." It became the basic element of official American tactics in negotiations concerning the future of Germany until 1944, and was strongly reaffirmed at Yalta in February, 1945. The military counterpart and facade for this political strategy was the unconditional surrender formula. As a war measure its superb virtue was that it preserved the unity of the "strange alliance" at a time when Soviet leaders were issuing vague but dark threats to make a separate peace with Hitler. Bickerings over peace terms might well have disrupted the "strange alliance." For the West, the policy held yet another, seldom remembered, advantage: it postponed crucial decisions about the future balance of power in Europe until after British and American armies were "heavily in France and Germany," as Harry Hopkins noted in March, 1943. As a war measure the formula was useful.

A Senior Fellow of the Research Institute on Communist Affairs of Columbia University and the author of several books, including *Meaning, Communication and Value* (1952), *Strategic Surrender: The Politics of Victory and Defeat* (1958), and *The Unexpected Revolution: Social Forces in the Hungarian Uprising* (1961), PAUL KECSKEMETI (b. 1901), like Armstrong, has analyzed the impact of the unconditional surrender policy on Germany. Unlike Armstrong, though, he does not think the public commitment to this formula for ending the war either discouraged Germans from resisting Hitler or encouraged them to prolong the fighting.*

Paul Kecskemeti

Of Little Impact

The refusal of the Germans to realize and digest defeat in World War I decisively influenced their thinking about ending hostilities in World War II. There was, for example, the official Nazi doctrine that defeat and capitulation were impossible. But the anti-Nazi opposition, too, started from the premise that the only alternative to victory was a negotiated peace. The opposition, however, rejected not only defeat but also victory. To them, victory was not only unlikely in view of the potential strength of the adversary, but unthinkable on moral grounds.

Among those who regarded a Nazi victory with moral revulsion were General Beck, Ambassador Ulrich von Hassell, Carl Gördeler (the former mayor of Leipzig), and their associates. Early in the war,

they desperately sought to establish contact with British (and American) circles, suggesting that they were ready to remove Hitler and then to conclude a moderate peace. Germany was to retain Hitler's "peaceful" conquests such as Austria and the Sudeten region; even the Polish Corridor was to remain in German possession; but the "new" Germany would observe international law and would be a trustworthy partner for the West. The first feelers of this type were put out in the period of the "phony war." Since no trial of strength had as yet taken place between Germany and the Anglo-French coalition, it is doubtful whether the Allies would have negotiated on such a basis, even if the opposition had succeeded in overthrowing Hitler. Neville Chamberlain, who knew

*From Paul Kecskemeti, *Strategic Surrender: The Politics of Victory and Defeat* (Stanford, Calif.: Stanford University Press, 1958), pp. 125–133, 223–228, 232–235. Reprinted by permission of The Rand Corporation. Footnotes omitted.

about the ideas of the German opposition, expressed his interest in purely academic terms.

More than a year later, after France had been knocked out of the war and Britain isolated, a similar offer was drafted by Carl Gördeler and forwarded through Swiss channels to London. This draft, dated May 30, 1941, contained the following main peace terms: Germany was to keep Alsace-Lorraine, the [Polish] Corridor and Danzig, Austria, the Sudeten region, and Memel; all other territories overrun by the German army were to be evacuated and returned to their pre-war status; Germany was to be given colonies under an international mandate system.

At the time this draft was written, Hitler's position seemed impregnable. He controlled Europe from the North Cape to the Aegean and the Pyrenees, and he was knocking at the gates of Suez. In this situation, Gördeler's proposals were moderate enough. But the war soon took a fateful turn for Germany with the invasion of Russia and the attack on Pearl Harbor, which ended Britain's isolation. A succession of defeats followed the string of early victories, but the opposition's peace platform remained substantially the same.

A second peace draft by Gördeler, written in the summer or fall of 1943 (but presumably never transmitted to the West), has been preserved. Its terms hardly differ from those of the first. Austria, the Sudeten region, and the Polish Corridor are still to remain German, and even South Tyrol is to be reannexed; the only major differences are that colonial demands are dropped and Alsace-Lorraine is to be either divided along linguistic lines or made independent.

It appears strange that, at a time when Germany was clearly losing the war, Gördeler still considered it possible that the Allies would accept a "Greater Germany."

The explanation for this lies partly in the Great German *mystique* that gripped Gördeler and his generation. To these Germans, it was axiomatic that no German-speaking population could remain outside the national domain. But Gördeler's terms are further explained by the fact that he was convinced that the Reich's political bargaining position was still strong enough, despite looming strategic defeat, to ensure acceptance of his program by the Allies. Moreover, a new factor had now gained prominence in the thinking of the opposition: they believed that the threat of massed Soviet legions in the east would bring it home to the Western Allies that they needed Germany as a bulwark against Russian and communist expansion. Now that military strength alone no longer afforded Germany a strong bargaining position, Gördeler and his group put their hopes in the latent tension between Russia and the West.

The logic of the situation made it impossible for the Western powers to insist on Germany's "unconditional surrender," once Hitler was removed. If Germany could not expect a negotiated peace on the basis of military strength alone, she could still reach the same objective as a result of the latent tension within the Allied camp. But this would be possible only if Hitler were removed quickly and peace overtures made while the German military position was still outwardly strong.

After Stalingrad, Gördeler circulated a memorandum among the German generals whose support he sought to win for his plans. The main argument of this paper follows [General] Ludendorff's thesis that when victory appears impossible, residual military strength must be used to obtain a negotiated peace, but Gördeler thought that Ludendorff erred in waiting too long. This mistake must not be repeated. . . .

For the circle around Beck and Gördeler,

the action for peace could not start early enough if Germany was to negotiate from strength. But they were unable to enlist the active support of the only group that was strong enough to move against Hitler—the active military leadership. Disaffected as the German generals mostly were, they simply could not bring themselves at this early stage to do anything that would diminish Germany's chances of military success. For the old-line generals, action against the political leadership became possible only when they had no doubt that the continuation of the war could only lead to strategic defeat.

In September 1943, Field Marshal von Kluge, who had formerly been reluctant to join the conspiracy against Hitler, came around to this point of view. The matter was discussed at a meeting in Berlin between Beck, Gördeler, and the Marshal. The British, Gördeler argued, would not insist on destroying Germany's might; they must be aware of the necessity of stopping Russian expansion. Kluge agreed: "It is high time," he said, "to act so as to exploit the military situation. . . . If an understanding is reached with the Anglo-Saxons, it is still possible to stabilize the eastern front east of the Polish borders and to make it impregnable." In answer to Gördeler's suggestion that the generals persuade Hitler to resign, Kluge argued in favor of assassinating the Führer.

This conversation, however, had no practical consequences. Shortly after his return to the eastern front, Kluge had an automobile accident that immobilized him for four months. A number of attempts on Hitler's life were made during this time, but none of them succeeded.

Readiness for action also crystallized among the military chiefs on the western front during the weeks preceding the Allied landing in Normandy. The landing, as the generals recognized, would lead to a two-front war; and in such a war Germany could only lose. To forestall this, the generals worked out a program for *selective* capitulation in the West only.

The details of this venture were described by General Speidel, Field Marshal Rommel's chief of staff. According to Speidel, in May 1944 Rommel and Generals von Stülpnagel and von Falkenhausen held a series of conferences at Rommel's headquarters. A plan was worked out, outlining the following course of action:

In the West: Definition of the premises under which an armistice could be concluded with Generals Eisenhower and Montgomery *without* participation by Hitler. . . .

The bases foreseen for negotiating an armistice were:

German evacuation of the occupied western territories and withdrawal behind the Westwall. Surrender of the administration of the occupied territories to the Allies. *Immediate suspension of the Allied bombing of Germany.* Armistice, not unconditional surrender, followed by negotiations for peace to bring about order and prevent chaos. Field Marshal Rommel expected that the Allies would give them such an opportunity. Appeal to the German people from all radio stations in the Western Command, frankly revealing the true political and military situation and its causes, and describing Hitler's criminal conduct of State affairs. Informing the troops of the measures necessary to avert a catastrophe.

The Home Front: Arrest of Hitler for trial before a German court by the resistance forces in the High Command of the Army, or rather by Panzer forces to be brought up for this purpose. . . .

In the East: Continuation of the fight. Holding a shortened line between the mouth of the Danube, the Carpathian mountains, Lemberg, the Vistula, and the Memel. Immediate evacuation of Courland (Lithuania) and other "fortresses."

The essential elements of this plan closely paralleled Gördeler's conception.

Here, too, the basic idea was that, once Germany got rid of Hitler, the Allies would be ready to grant her favorable terms and would welcome active German assistance against the communist peril. On the method to be followed, too, the generals adhered to the Ludendorff-Gördeler line. An armistice was to be proposed before the invasion began. "For all negotiations," Speidel says, "a firm western front was a prerequisite. The stability of the western front was, therefore, our constant concern."

The generals' plan eventually came to nothing; there is no evidence that they even attempted to contact General Eisenhower, and they did nothing to arrest and try Hitler. All Rommel did was to send an "ultimative" memorandum to Hitler on July 15, calling on him to "draw the conclusions" from the fact that the war was lost. Kluge was now in the West, having succeeded Rundstedt as commander in chief. . . . He had actively joined the conspiracy a few months earlier. Summoned by the conspirators to act, he declined, saying that he was not sure whether his subordinates would obey him.

The military catastrophes of the summer of 1944 (the Allied breakthrough in France and the simultaneous rupture of the eastern front in Poland) had a shattering effect on the opposition. They destroyed the basis of Gördeler's conception, negotiation from strength. In terms of his theory, it was too late to act. On July 12 Beck told one of the conspirators, Gisevius, that he thought the right moment for attacking Hitler had been missed. Germany's total occupation could no longer be prevented.

Before these military disasters it had been hard for the Beck-Gördeler circle to recognize that hostilities could only be ended on the basis of surrender. This had been clear to Gisevius since long before mid-1944: he did

not believe that the Allied demand for "unconditional surrender" could be disregarded. For him, then, the only possibility was to make the surrender as "selective" as possible, by sucking the Allies into German territory before the Russians entered. In the spring of 1944, Beck and Gördeler finally came around to the same position. They tried to find out through Gisevius, who had contacts with Allen W. Dulles in Switzerland, whether the Americans would accept unilateral surrender from an anti-Nazi German government. The conspirators may have thought that the Allies' attitude toward Germany would change after a new German government offered capitulation to them. They contemplated making an offer of active military help to the Allies, including assistance for the landing of parachute troops in Germany. This is how [historian Gerhard] Ritter sums up the situation:

It is clear that the leaders of the opposition were now [spring, 1944] virtually ready to accept the formula of "unconditional surrender" vis-à-vis the Western powers, confident, to be sure, that sober political reason would overcome the stark will to destruction in the latter's camp and that the common interest in preserving Western civilization would assert itself and save the German state from total destruction. They evidently had in mind, not an armistice with a shortened western front line . . . but a kind of merger of German and Anglo-Saxon units, or at least immediate occupation of Germany from the west, before the Red armies had overrun Poland and reached the Reich's borders. Peace negotiations were then to follow between victors and vanquished, but with a new German government to whom the victors would owe a substantial shortening of the final phase of hostilities, and whom they had pledged to recognize.

In the end, then, the German opposition did work out a terminal strategy of "disarming" the winner. But the strategy could not be applied because of the failure of the coup against Hitler. Even if the coup had been successful, it is uncertain how much the strategy of "disarming" would have achieved. The Allies were unwilling to recognize any latent conflict of interest with Soviet Russia. Their reaction to the German opposition's earlier appeals, appeals that had made much of the danger of bolshevization, had been completely negative. . . .

The unconditional-surrender policy has been severely criticized on the ground that it needlessly prolonged the war. The demand for unconditional surrender, it is argued, rallied the German people behind the war regime and induced them to fight to the last. Faced with the demand for unconditional surrender, which was tantamount to the annihilation of their national existence, the Germans and the other Axis powers had no choice but to fight as long as was physically possible. If a less severe formula had been used in Allied war propaganda, or even if very severe but specified surrender terms had been offered, resistance would have come to an end sooner.

The criticism clearly refers to the negative, "anti-Wilsonian" phase of the unconditional-surrender policy. It is undeniable that the formula, when it was launched, furnished ammunition to Nazi war propaganda. Göbbels made copious use of it to counteract the disastrous effects on morale of the defeats Germany suffered in Africa and at Stalingrad. But this alone does not prove that the unconditional-surrender policy prolonged German resistance.

That the war would have been shorter if the Allies' basic war aim had not been total victory is, of course, true. Ending the war by a negotiated peace would have resulted in a shorter war and possibly in a better political situation after the war. But few critics maintain that this would have been the correct policy. Most critics, rather, take the objective of total victory for granted and argue that it would have been attained more quickly and more easily if a more positive formula than unconditional surrender had been used.

[The writer J.F.C.] Fuller, for example, maintains that "the Allied policy of unconditional surrender, by deliberately preventing the surrender of Germany on terms, could mean but one of two things to every German—either victory or annihilation."

Actual German behavior during the latter part of the war, however, cannot be squared with this judgment. For Hitler, annihilation was indeed the only alternative to victory, but not because surrender on terms was ruled out by the Allies. The Nazis' official doctrine of the war did not allow for surrender on terms. On the other hand, there were many Germans who saw that the war was lost but who refused to admit that this necessarily meant total national extinction. They looked to a third alternative, recognizing that the solution lay in ending the hopeless struggle by capitulation if necessary. Although it certainly cannot be said that they acquiesced in unconditional surrender, it would be equally wrong to maintain that "surrender on terms" was the only formula to which such Germans would subscribe. As we have seen in the case study of the German surrender, there was no German last-ditch resistance inspired by the feeling, "If you accept surrender on terms, all right, but if you refuse to do so, nothing remains for us to do but go down fighting to the last." . . .

The major stumbling block in the way of an active surrender policy was the fact that, as long as Hitler was commander in chief, no military leader could initiate surrender without becoming guilty of flagrant insubordination. To the typical officer surrender was well-nigh unthinkable, no matter how senseless and suicidal continued resistance appeared to him. Germans had to choose between military rationality, which implied surrender, and military loyalty, which involved continued resistance. For the military leaders, the latter was a moral imperative. In determining their choice, all purely political questions, including unconditional surrender, played a lesser role. The authors of the July 1944 plot certainly hoped to obtain qualified surrender, despite the Allies' verbal insistence on unconditional surrender. They did not conclude from the unconditional-surrender policy that they had no alternative but to continue a hopeless struggle. Those Germans who at that time chose to fight to the end did so more because they could not bring themselves to break faith with the Führer than because of Allied statements.

As pointed out above, German terminal resistance was selective—stubborn in the East, almost nonexistent in the West. Had the slogan of unconditional surrender made all the difference between last-ditch resistance and surrender, this selective resistance could not have happened, especially since the Western Allies practically had a copyright on the slogan. The Russians used mostly themes other than unconditional surrender in their propaganda in Germany. Stalin used the formula in his order of the day of May 1, 1943, in order to allay Allied uneasiness about his seductive propaganda to the Germans, but later (notably in his speech of November 6, 1943) he again reverted to an appealing language that was in open contrast to the Allied handling of the theme of surrender. If use of the slogan was a propagandistic blunder, the Russians largely avoided it, but their sagacity in this respect was by no

means rewarded. It was the Western Allies who obtained the advantage of slackening final resistance by Germany.

This indicates that the generally assumed causal relationship between the *formula* of unconditional surrender and the length of the war is illusory. The length of the war was determined largely by other factors, including the Allies' objective of total victory and Hitler's (and the Japanese war extremists') refusal to admit the possibility of any kind of surrender. The terminal behavior of the Germans also indicates that unconditional surrender to the Western Allies was not unthinkable for them; it was the loss of German territory to the Russians that they viewed as the ultimate catastrophe. Lord Hankey's statement, "Not one of the German leaders was willing to sign such humiliating terms as unconditional surrender," is directly contradicted by the facts: both anti-Nazi dissidents and Nazi loyalists were willing to do just that, as our case study of the German surrender shows.

Fuller propounds the thesis that the announced policy of unconditional surrender was the reason that hostilities did not end quickly after strategic decision had been reached in the West:

In a sane war, Rundstedt's defeat in the Ardennes would have brought hostilities to an immediate end; but because of unconditional surrender the war was far from being sane. Gagged by this idiotic slogan, the Western Allies could offer no terms, however severe. Conversely, their enemy could ask for none, however submissive.

General Westphal, however, who was Rundstedt's chief of staff during the war, reviewed the terminal situation as it appeared from the German side and made the following comment:

Yet, it is said, at least he [Rundstedt] could have stopped the fighting in the West and capitulated. He would have been only too willing to make an end to the mounting losses of men and the destruction of even more German cities from the air. Should he then make contact of his own accord with Eisenhower? His military upbringing ruled that out. Perhaps nowadays these basic principles are thought to be out of date. But no one can jump over his own shadow.

In the next sentence, Westphal mentions "unconditional surrender" as an additional reason why Rundstedt could not offer capitulation. But this had nothing to do with the harshness of the formula. The western front had to be held, Westphal says, in order to "defend the rear of the army in the east." Capitulation in the West had to be ruled out, otherwise "the front against the Russians would necessarily collapse also." Had it not been for this consequence, capitulation by the field commanders would have been clearly indicated, where it was not rejected out of loyalty to their superiors. . . .

What the record indicates is that the mere verbal expression of Allied policy exercised no major influence upon the stubbornness of enemy resistance and the duration of the war. The belief that the Allies could have shortened the war appreciably if they had mitigated the excesses of their verbal behavior is a myth. This myth is readily believed because it is consonant with one of the pervasive beliefs of our age, the belief in manipulation as the main factor determining human conduct. Addicted to a naïve stimulus-response philosophy, we tend to take it for granted that people's actions depend on nothing but the momentary stimuli they receive, stimuli that we, the manipulators, can control at will. Where this philosophy holds sway, the possibility that conduct might also have other sources is not even taken into consideration. There is no room for the "autono-

mous" sources of conduct in the simplistic philosophy that colors so much of our present political thinking. Accordingly, during the war, the enemy's own permanent and deep-rooted loyalties, his own spontaneous assessment of his interests, and similar autonomous factors were not taken into account when we tried to foresee and influence his conduct in the terminal situation. Nothing seemed to matter except what we did to him and what we told him then and there. Even in retrospect, we indulge in fantasies to the effect that everything would have happened differently if our verbal manipulation of the enemy's actions had been more skillful. This line of criticism is worthless because it is based upon the manipulative fallacy, a misconception that the critics share with the policymakers whose decisions they scrutinize.

There is, however, an even more fundamental flaw in this kind of criticism of the unconditional-surrender policy. The main question to which it is addressed, namely, whether the policy of unconditional surrender has "prolonged the war," is irrelevant. This sort of question was centrally relevant to the assessment of the merits of basic strategic decisions in World War I, where it turned out in retrospect that victory, though fully achieved, had no real, lasting value for the principal winners, France and England, because they had bled themselves white in pursuing it. The drain on their resources involved in coming out of the war in possession of a complete monopoly of armed strength turned out to be more important in the long run than that monopoly itself. For France and Britain, victory was Pyrrhic because the war "lasted too long"; i.e., it was too costly in lives and material goods. The victory the West achieved in World War II also turned out to be hollow, but not owing to the length or costliness of the war as such. The war, of course, had been tremendously destructive, and it may well be argued that the political aftermath would have been better if the Allies had been less adamant in ruling out political concessions to new, regenerate regimes on the enemy side. But it was not the undue prolongation of the war that was primarily responsible for the hollowness of the victory, nor was the excessive length and destructiveness of the war caused by the lack of a sensible strategic concept on the eventual winners' side.

In World War I, the West's holding out for complete victory was ill-advised because it entailed exhaustion. For this reason alone, a policy of compromise would have been preferable. (It is not inconceivable, though it is by no means certain, that a compromise settlement could have been worked out with Germany.) In World War II, however, the western conduct of operations at least did not involve the insane strategic concept of symmetrical, mutual attrition, i.e., months and years of almost uninterrupted slaughter, "justified" by the hope of still having some divisions left when the enemy had none. The West's attrition strategy in World War II was more destructive than it need

have been, but at least it was, by and large, asymmetrical, as a genuine winning strategy must be. For the United States, politically the leading power of the West, the war had not been total at all, and if the postwar period found the West in a politically disadvantageous position, it was not because the human and economic substance of its leading component had been drained away. Nor was the West's political intransigence the chief reason why fighting continued far beyond the point where strategic victory was assured: blindness and fanaticism on the eventual losers' side would probably have led to this result even if the eventual winners had been less intransigent.

It seems, then, that fastening upon the "unnecessary prolongation" of the war as the main criterion of weakness in the Allied war leadership is just one more instance of the well-known tendency of strategic thinking to lag one war behind. As we have seen above, the unconditional-surrender policy itself was conceived largely in an effort to avoid a supposed mistake made in the previous war; its critics, however, are apparently not above falling into similar errors.

One of the most well-known spokesmen for the revisionist case against American diplomacy at Yalta is the journalist WILLIAM HENRY CHAMBERLIN (b. 1897). A correspondent in Moscow and the Far East for many years and more recently a columnist for the *Wall Street Journal*, Chamberlin is also the author of several books, including *America's Second Crusade* (1950), a study of the origins and course of World War II. Depicting Franklin Roosevelt in this volume and other writings as incredibly naïve, Chamberlin describes American wartime diplomacy under Roosevelt, particularly at Yalta, as "intellectual, moral, political, and economic bankruptcy, complete and irretrievable."*

William Henry Chamberlin

A Pro-Russian Fiasco

The second conference of the Big Three, held at Yalta in February 1945, represented the high point of Soviet diplomatic success and correspondingly the low point of American appeasement. This conference took place under circumstances which were very disadvantageous to the western powers.

Roosevelt's mental and physical condition had disquieted Stimson ... [in September 1944] when the Morgenthau Plan was being approved. It certainly did not improve as a result of the strenuous presidential campaign and the long trip to the Crimean resort.

There has been no authoritative uninhibited analysis of the state of the President's health during the war. But there is

a good deal of reliable testimony of serious deterioration, especially during the last year of Mr. Roosevelt's life. And it was during this year that decisions of the most vital moral and political importance had to be taken. . . .

Roosevelt went to Yalta with no prepared agenda and no clearly defined purpose, except to get along with Stalin at any price. He had been provided with a very complete file of studies and recommendations, drawn up by the State Department, before he boarded the heavy cruiser *Quincy*, which took him to Malta, where there was a break in the journey to the Crimea. But these were never looked at. The President suffered from a cold and from sinus trouble and his appearance "disturbed" James F.

---

*From William Henry Chamberlin, *America's Second Crusade* (Chicago: Henry Regnery Company, 1950), pp. 206, 208–220. Footnotes omitted.

Byrnes, who accompanied him on this trip.

The conference at Yalta lasted a week, from February 4 until February 11, 1945. The principal subjects discussed were Poland, German boundaries and reparations, the occupation regime for Germany, the conditions of Soviet participation in the war against Japan, procedure and voting rights in the future United Nations organization.

At the price of a few promises which were soon to prove worthless in practice, Stalin got what he wanted in Poland: a frontier that assigned to the Soviet Union almost half of Poland's prewar territory and the abandonment by America and Great Britain of the Polish government-in-exile in London. Roosevelt made a feeble plea that Lwów and the adjacent oil fields be included in Poland. Churchill appealed to Stalin's sense of generosity. Neither achieved any success.

On the German question Churchill took a stand for moderation. Stalin recommended that the western frontier of Poland should be extended to the Neisse River, bringing large tracts of ethnic German territory under Polish rule. Churchill suggested that it would be a pity to stuff the Polish goose so full of German food that he would die of indigestion.

The British Premier privately estimated to Byrnes that nine million Germans would be displaced by giving Poland a frontier on the Neisse River and that such a number could never be absorbed. It is the Neisse River that marks the Polish-German frontier in 1950, although the Yalta communiqué merely stated that "Poland must receive substantial accessions of territory in the North and West."

There was agreement in principle that Germany should be broken up into separate states. However, no positive decision was adopted. The matter was referred to the European Advisory Commission, composed of American, British, and Soviet representatives sitting in London. Here it died a natural death. The dismemberment of Germany was not discussed at the next major conference, at Potsdam.

The Soviet representatives at Yalta had large and fairly precise ideas as to what they wished to take from Germany as reparations. They wanted to remove physically 80 per cent of Germany's heavy industries and also to receive deliveries in kind for ten years. Churchill recalled the unsuccessful experience with reparations after the last war and spoke of "the spectre of an absolutely starving Germany". Ivan Maisky, Soviet spokesman on this question, proposed that reparations be fixed at the figure of twenty billion dollars, with the Soviet Union to receive at least half of this sum.

Roosevelt had little to suggest on this subject, except to remark that the United States would have no money to send into Germany for food, clothing, and housing. It was finally decided to leave the details to a reparations commission. There was no firm promise on America's part to support a Soviet claim for ten billion dollars in reparations, although the Soviet Government, with its usual tendency to lose nothing for want of asking for it, later tried to represent that there had been such a commitment.

If one considers the value of the territory lost by Germany in the East, the prodigious looting, organized and unorganized, carried out by the Red Army, and the system in the Soviet zone of occupation under which a large share of German industrial output is siphoned off for Soviet use, it is probable that Germany was stripped of assets considerably in excess of ten billion dollars in value.

The protocol on reparations mentioned "the use of labor" as a possible source of reparations. Roosevelt observed that "the

United States cannot take man power as the Soviet Republic can." This gave implied American sanction to the large-scale exploitation of German war prisoners as slave labor in Britain and France, as well as in Russia, after the end of the war. The Morgenthau Plan, which Roosevelt and Churchill had approved at Quebec, recommended "forced German labor outside Germany" as a form of reparations.

Procedure in the United Nations was discussed at some length. The records show that Roosevelt and Churchill were as unwilling as Stalin to forego the right of veto in serious disputes, where the use of armed force was under discussion. There was a dispute, not settled at Yalta, as to whether the right of veto should apply to discussion of controversial matters. The Russians insisted that it should, the western representatives contended that it should not. Stalin conceded this minor point when Harry Hopkins visited Moscow in June 1945.

The Soviet Government received Roosevelt's consent to its proposal that Byelorussia and the Ukraine, two of the affiliated Soviet republics, should be granted individual votes in the United Nations Assembly. When Byrnes learned of this he raised vigorous objection, reminding Roosevelt that some of the opposition to America's entrance into the League of Nations was based on the argument that Britain would have five votes, one for each member of the Commonwealth. Roosevelt then asked for and obtained Stalin's consent to an arrangement which would give the United States three votes in the Assembly. This compensation was never pressed for and did not go into effect.

In reason and logic there was no case for giving separate votes to the Ukraine and Byelorussia. If the Soviet Union was a loose federation of independent states, like the British Commonwealth, each of its sixteen constituent republics should have been entitled to a vote. If it was a centralized unitary state, it should have received only one vote. No one with an elementary knowledge of Soviet political realities could doubt that the Soviet Union belongs in the second category. It would cause no special shock or surprise to see Canada, South Africa, Australia, or India voting in opposition to Britain on some issues. It would be unthinkable for the Ukraine or Byelorussia to oppose the Soviet Union. . . .

In Yugoslavia, as in Poland, the Yalta Agreement provided a screen of fair words behind which the friends of the West were ruthlessly liquidated. It was decided to recommend that a new government be formed on the basis of agreement between Tito and Subasic. The antifascist Assembly of National Liberation (an organization of Tito's predominantly Communist followers) was to be enlarged by the addition of members of the last Yugoslav parliament who "had not compromised themselves by collaboration with the enemy." Legislative acts passed by the Assembly were to be subject to ratification by a constituent assembly.

All this sounded fair enough. What it meant in practice was that two non-Communists, Subasic and Grol, joined Tito's regime, the former as Foreign Minister, the latter as Vice-Premier. But their tenure of office was precarious and brief. Grol's newspaper was suppressed and he resigned from the government in August 1945, accusing the regime of a long series of violations of elementary political and civil liberties. Subasic followed his example soon afterwards and was placed under house arrest.

And Tito's constituent assembly was chosen under an electoral law "which rendered the very appearance of a candidate's name on the opposition list a danger to that candidate's life." The "new democracy", so very like the old fascism in psychology and methods, marched on to further victories. Yalta put the seal on the process which had begun at Teheran of betraying the East Europeans who preferred free institutions to communism. All that followed, or could follow, was a long series of futile diplomatic protests from Washington and London.

Another country was offered up as a sacrifice on the altar of appeasement at Yalta. This was China. Stalin had told Hull at Moscow and Roosevelt at Teheran that he would be on the side of the United States and Great Britain against Japan after the end of the war with Germany. At Yalta, with German military collapse clearly impending, the Soviet dictator set a price for his intervention in the Far East. The price was stiff. And it included items which it was not morally justifiable for the United States to accept. The Big Three agreed that

the former rights of Russia, violated by the treacherous attack of Japan in 1904, shall be restored, viz.:

(a) The southern part of Sakhalin as well as the islands adjacent to it shall be returned to the Soviet Union;

(b) The commercial port of Dairen shall be internationalized, the pre-eminent interest of the Soviet Union in this port being safeguarded and the lease of Port Arthur as a naval base of the Soviet Union restored.

(c) The Chinese Eastern Railway, and the South Manchuria Railway, which provide an outlet to Dairen, shall be jointly operated by the establishment of a joint Soviet-Chinese company, it being understood that the pre-eminent interests of the Soviet Union shall be safeguarded and that China shall retain full sovereignty in Manchuria.

The Kurile Islands, a long chain of barren, volcanic islands extending into the North Pacific northeast of Japan proper, were to be handed over to the Soviet Union. The *status quo* was to be preserved

in Outer Mongolia, a huge, sparsely populated, arid region which the Soviet Union took over without formal annexation in 1924.

South Sakhalin (which had belonged to Russia until 1905) and the Kurile Islands might be regarded as war booty, to be taken from Japan. And China had no prospect of upsetting *de facto* Soviet rule of Outer Mongolia by its own strength. But the concessions which Roosevelt and Churchill made to Stalin in Manchuria were of fateful importance for China's independence and territorial integrity.

Manchuria, because of its natural wealth in coal, iron, soya beans, and other resources, and because of the large investment of Japanese capital and technical skill, intensified after 1931, was the most industrially developed part of China. To give a strong foreign power control over its railways, a predominant interest in its chief port, Dairen, and a naval base at Port Arthur was to sign away China's sovereignty in Manchuria.

And this was done not only without consulting China but without informing China. The Chinese Government was prevented from even discussing Soviet claims in the future. For, at Stalin's insistence, the agreement to satisfy his annexationist claims was put in writing and contained this decisive assurance:

"The Heads of the three Great Powers have agreed that these claims of the Soviet Union shall be unquestioningly fulfilled after Japan has been defeated."

In the opinion of former Ambassador William C. Bullitt "no more unnecessary, disgraceful and potentially disastrous document has ever been signed by a President of the United States."

Severe as this judgment sounds, it has been borne out by the course of subsequent events. The Soviet intervention in the Far Eastern war was of no military benefit to the United States, because it took place only a few days before Japan surrendered. Politically this intervention was an unmitigated disaster.

During the Soviet occupation of Manchuria industrial equipment of an estimated value of two billion dollars was looted and carried off to Russia. This delayed for a long time any prospect of Chinese industrial self-sufficiency. As soon as Soviet troops occupied Manchuria, Chinese Communist forces, as if by a mysterious signal, began to converge on that area.

The Soviet military commanders shrewdly avoided direct, ostentatious cooperation with the Communists. After all, the Soviet Government had signed a treaty of friendship and alliance with the Nationalist Government of China on August 14, 1945. One clause of this treaty prescribed that "the Soviet Government is ready to render China moral support and assistance with military equipment and other material resources, this support and assistance to be given fully to the National Government as the central government of China."

This treaty was to prove about as valuable to the cosignatory as the nonaggression pacts which the Soviet Government concluded with Poland, Finland, Latvia, Lithuania, and Estonia. There is no indication that the Soviet Government gave the slightest "moral" or material support to the Chinese Nationalist Government. But Manchuria became an arsenal for the Chinese Communists, who were able to equip themselves with Japanese arms, obligingly stacked up for them by the Soviet occupation forces.

Soviet control of Dairen was used to block the use of this important port by Nationalist troops. Manchuria became the base from which the Chinese Communists could launch a campaign that led to the overrunning of almost all China.

Roosevelt's concessions at Yalta represented an abandonment of the historic policy of the United States in the Far East. This policy was in favor of the "open door", of equal commercial opportunity for all foreign nations, together with respect for Chinese independence. The American State Department had always been opposed to the "closed door" methods of Imperial Russia.

But at Yalta the "open door" was abandoned in a document that repeatedly referred to "the pre-eminent interests of the Soviet Union" in Manchuria. Those interests have now become pre-eminent in China. And the surrender of Manchuria to Stalin is not the least of the reasons for this development.

The Yalta concessions were a violation of the American pledge at Cairo that Manchuria should be restored to China. If New York State had been occupied by an enemy and was then handed back to the United States on condition that another alien power should have joint control of its railway systems, a predominant voice in the Port of New York Authority, and the right to maintain a naval base on Staten Island, most Americans would not feel that American sovereignty had been respected.

Whether considered from the standpoint of consistency with professed war aims or from the standpoint of serving American national interests, the record of Yalta is profoundly depressing. The large-scale alienation of Polish territory to the Soviet Union, of German territory to Poland, constituted an obvious and flagrant violation of the self-determination clauses of the Atlantic Charter. An offensive note of hypocrisy was added by inserting into the Yalta communiqué repeated professions of adherence to the Atlantic Charter.

The hopes of tens of millions of East Europeans for national independence and personal liberty were betrayed. The leaders of the Axis could scarcely have surpassed the cynicism of Roosevelt and Churchill in throwing over allies like Poland and China. The unwarranted concessions to Stalin in the Far East opened a Pandora's Box of troubles for the United States, the end of which has not yet been seen.

There was not one positive, worth-while contribution to European revival and stability in the sordid deals of Yalta, only imperialist power politics at its worst. The vindictive peace settlement, far worse than that of Versailles, which was being prepared promised little for European reconstruction. Roosevelt not long before had piously declared that "the German people are not going to be enslaved, because the United Nations do not traffic in human slavery." But at Yalta he sanctioned the use of the slave labor of German war prisoners, a throwback to one of the most barbarous practices of antiquity.

The agreements, published and secret, concluded at Yalta are defended mainly on two grounds. It is contended that military necessity forced the President to comply with Stalin's demands in Eastern Europe and East Asia. It is also argued that the source of difficulties in postwar Europe is to be found, not in the Yalta agreements, but in the Soviet failure to abide by these agreements.

Neither of these justifications stands up under serious examination. America in February 1945 was close to the peak of its military power. The atomic bomb still lay a few months in the future. But the United States possessed the most powerful navy in the world, the greatest aircraft production in quantity and quality, an army that, with its British and other allies, had swept the Germans from North Africa, France, Belgium, and much of Italy.

The lumbering Soviet offensive in the East was dependent in no small degree on lend-lease American trucks and communication equipment. There was, therefore, no good reason for approaching Stalin with an inferiority complex or for consenting to a Polish settlement which sacrificed the friends of the West in that country and paved the way for the establishment of a Soviet puppet regime.

No doubt Stalin could have imposed such a regime by force. Only the Red Army in February 1945 was in a position to occupy Poland. How much better the outlook would have been if Churchill's repeated prodding for action in the Balkans had been heeded, if the Polish Army of General Anders, battle-hardened in Italy, had been able to reach Poland ahead of the Red Army!

But there would have been a great difference between a Soviet stooge regime set up by the naked force of the Red Army and one strengthened by the acquiescence and endorsement of the western powers. The former would have enjoyed no shred of moral authority. As it was, nationalist guerrilla resistance to the made-in-Moscow government was prolonged and embittered. Many thousands of lives were lost on both sides before the satellite regime, with a good deal of Russian military and police aid, clamped down its rule more or less effectively over the entire country. How much stronger this resistance would have been if the United States and Great Britain had continued to recognize the government-in-exile and insisted on adequate guarantees of free and fair elections!

There was equally little reason to give in to Stalin's Far Eastern demands. The desire to draw the Soviet Union into this war was fatuous, from the standpoint of America's interest in a truly independent China. Apparently Roosevelt was the victim of some extremely bad intelligence work. He was given to understand that the Kwantung Army, the Japanese occupation force in Manchuria, was a formidable fighting machine, which might be used to resist the

American invasion of the Japanese home islands which was planned for the autumn.

But the Kwantung Army offered no serious resistance to the Soviet invasion in August. It had evidently been heavily depleted in numbers and lowered in fighting quality.

Apologists for the Yalta concessions maintain that Japan in February 1945 presented the aspect of a formidable, unbeaten enemy. Therefore, so the argument runs, Roosevelt was justified in paying a price for Soviet intervention, in the interest of ending the war quickly and saving American lives.

But Japanese resistance to American air and naval attacks on its own coasts was already negligible. American warships were able to cruise along the shores of Japan, bombarding at will. According to an account later published by Arthur Krock, of the *New York Times,* an Air Force general presented a report at Yalta pointing to the complete undermining of the Japanese capacity to resist. But the mistaken and misleading view that Japan still possessed powerful military and naval force prevailed.

Acceptance of this view by Roosevelt was especially unwarranted because two days before he left for Yalta Roosevelt received from General MacArthur a forty-page message outlining five unofficial Japanese peace overtures which amounted to an acceptance of unconditional surrender, with the sole reservation that the Emperor should be preserved. The other terms offered by the Japanese, who were responsible men, in touch with Emperor Hirohito, may be summarized as follows:

1. Complete surrender of all Japanese forces.

2. Surrender of all arms and munitions.

3. Occupation of the Japanese homeland and island possessions by Allied troops under American direction.

4. Japanese relinquishment of Manchu-

ria, Korea, and Formosa, as well as all territory seized during the war.

5. Regulation of Japanese industry to halt present and future production of implements of war.

6. Turning over of any Japanese the United States might designate as war criminals.

7. Immediate release of all prisoners of war and internees in Japan and areas under Japanese control.

MacArthur recommended negotiations on the basis of the Japanese overtures. But Roosevelt brushed off this suggestion with the remark: "MacArthur is our greatest general and our poorest politician."

That the President, after receiving such a clear indication that Japan was on the verge of military collapse, should have felt it necessary to bribe Stalin into entering the Far Eastern war must surely be reckoned a major error of judgment, most charitably explained by Roosevelt's failing mental and physical powers.

Captain Ellis M. Zacharias, Navy expert on Japan whose broadcasts in fluent Japanese hastened the surrender, asserts that intelligence reports indicating Japanese impending willingness to surrender were available at the time of the Yalta Conference.

One such report, communicated in the utmost secrecy to an American intelligence officer in a neutral capital, predicted the resignation of General Koiso as Premier in favor of the pacific Admiral Suzuki. The Admiral, in turn, according to the report, would turn over power to the Imperial Prince Higashi Kuni, who would possess sufficient authority and prestige, backed by a command from the Emperor, to arrange the surrender.

I am convinced that had this document, later proven to be correct in every detail, been brought to the attention of President Roosevelt and his military advisers, the war might have been viewed in a different light, both Iwo Jima and Okinawa might have been avoided, and different decisions could have been reached at Yalta.

Zacharias also believes that if the Japanese had been given a precise definition of what America understood by unconditional surrender as late as June, or even at the end of July 1945, both Soviet intervention and the dropping of atomic bombs on Hiroshima and Nagasaki could have been averted.

Certainly there was a hopeful alternative to the policy, so disastrous in its results, of encouraging and bribing the Soviet Union to enter the Far Eastern picture. This was to aim at a quick peace with Japan, before the Soviet armies could have been transferred from the West to the East. There is every reason to believe that such a peace was attainable, if the Japanese had been assured of the right to keep the Emperor and perhaps given some assurance that their commercial interests in Manchuria and Korea would not be entirely wiped out.

There is little weight in the contention that the Yalta agreements, in themselves, were excellent, if the Soviet Government had only lived up to them. These agreements grossly violated the Atlantic Charter by assigning Polish territory to the Soviet Union and German territory to Poland without plebiscites. They violated the most elementary rules of humanity and civilized warfare by sanctioning slave labor as "reparations". And the whole historic basis of American foreign policy in the Far East was upset by the virtual invitation to Stalin to take over Japan's former exclusive and dominant role in Manchuria.

The Chamberlin view of American diplomacy at Yalta has been repeatedly challenged in the years since the close of World War II, and this in turn has produced other writings emphasizing many of Chamberlin's points. To help settle this controversy, the Historical Division of the Department of State published *The Conferences at Malta and Yalta*, a thousand-page volume of documents, in 1955. Yet in spite of this publication, the argument has continued with each side finding confirmation for its assumptions in the documentary record. A good example of how Chamberlin's arguments have been answered comes from the pen of SIDNEY WARREN (b. 1916), a professor of political science at California Western University and the author of books and articles on the American presidency.*

Sidney Warren

A Realistic Response
to International Conditions

The ring of steel that the coalition had been battling to draw around Germany began to close and throttle the Nazis by the beginning of 1945. An offensive in the West had liberated France, Brussels, and Antwerp, and Allied troops were approaching the Rhine. At the same time on the Eastern front, Soviet troops had crashed out of Russian territory to occupy a line extending all the way from the Baltic to the Balkans; by February, they were only forty-five miles from Berlin. With victory in sight, such matters as the coordination of final military operations, the nature of the German occupation, and a common strategy for the war against Japan required an early settlement. Moreover, the differences that the Allies had submerged for the sake of military unity were mount-ing to the surface to threaten the Grand Alliance.

At Roosevelt's request, another Big Three conference was arranged to meet at Yalta in the Russian Crimea, at which he hoped they could resolve their differences. For eight days, from February 4 to February 11, 1945, the three heads of state grappled with momentous issues. Their decisions would affect the politics of the world for generations to come. Major items on the agenda were the future of Germany, the governments of Poland and other East European countries, the Far East settlement, and the United Nations organization.

This was the last meeting of the Big Three; two months later, Roosevelt would be gone, struck down by a cerebral hemor-

---

*From the book *The President as World Leader* by Sidney Warren. Copyright © 1964 by Sidney Warren. Reprinted by permission of J. B. Lippincott Company. Pp. 259–269.

rhage which took his life. The great hopes he had encouraged for a future of peace and justice already had begun to wither. Disillusionment with the diplomacy of Yalta was evident even before he passed from the scene. In the years that followed, critics laid at the door of the President, because of his negotiations at that conference, almost all the problems which have afflicted the world since the defeat of the Axis.

It has been charged that Roosevelt was already a dying man and no longer alert when he participated in the deliberations. While he was worn and exhausted—the nation was shocked by his gaunt and frail appearance when he returned from the Crimea—the records of the conference show conclusively that his mental acuteness was unimpaired. Nor were the famed buoyancy, charm, and humor absent. The President's deteriorating health was entirely inconsequential as a factor influencing the decisions. Settlements hammered out at Yalta reflected not only Roosevelt's judgments but those of his diplomatic and military advisers, high-ranking officers in the State Department, as well as of Prime Minister Churchill and his staff.

Another unfounded accusation is that the President went to the conference unprepared. On the contrary, Roosevelt and his new Secretary of State, Edward R. Stettinius, Jr., devoted considerable time and thought in advance of the meeting to formulating a program and achieving a harmony of views with the British. Stettinius conducted an extensive briefing session in French Morocco with his staff, then went on to Malta, where he was joined by the President for detailed discussions with Churchill and Eden before they all left for Yalta. A comparison of the pre-conference briefing papers prepared by the State Department with the minutes of the Yalta proceedings reveals that Roosevelt was thoroughly familiar with the major policy statements contained in those documents.

Rarely in recent times has the leader of a democratic state been blamed for so much. Roosevelt has been charged with surrendering Eastern Europe and its peoples to Soviet hegemony and with perpetrating a monstrous sell-out of the Far East. Much of the indictment, however, has been made with the omniscience of hindsight and without taking into account the situation as it existed in 1945. With regard to Europe, the conference was held at a time when circumstances militated against advantageous territorial and political decisions for the West. The Allies had not yet bridged the Rhine, the advance in Italy had bogged down in the Apennines, and the troops were still staggering from blows they had received in the Battle of the Bulge. Soviet troops, on the other hand, were triumphantly hurling back the Nazis. They had just swept through almost all of Poland and East Prussia, had at some points reached the Oder River in Germany, and had captured most of Hungary while the Yugoslav Partisans had retaken Belgrade. Except for Czechoslovakia, all of Eastern Europe was thus in the hands of the Red Army. It was, therefore, not a question of what Churchill and Roosevelt would permit Stalin to do, but what they could persuade him to accept. George F. Kennan, veteran diplomat and historian, later commented, "The establishment of Soviet military power in Eastern Europe ... was not the result of [Yalta]" but of military operations. "There was nothing the western democracies could have done to prevent the Russians from entering those areas except to get there first, and this they were not in a position to do."

In connection with the Far East, one of Roosevelt's major objectives at Yalta was committing the Russians to an early date for entering the war against Japan. The bloody campaign in the Pacific to eject the Japanese island by island was still in progress, and plans had been projected for a major invasion of the country in the fall of 1945. Secretary Stimson recorded that, in the War Department's judgment, Japan would probably resist to the end in all the areas under her control. "In such an event," he wrote, "the Allies would be faced with the enormous task of destroying an armed force of five million men and five thousand suicide aircraft belonging to a race which had . . . demonstrated its ability to fight literally to the death. . . . I was informed that such operations might be expected to cost over a million casualties to American forces alone." With the help of the Soviet Union countless American lives would be saved, and all the President's advisers were agreed that the United States dare not go it alone against Japan. The atom bomb had not yet been tested. Not for another five months would word come from Los Alamos that the experiment had succeeded.

Still another consideration motivated the President throughout the involved discussions. He was convinced that peace could not endure in the postwar world without Soviet cooperation, which he believed could be obtained by making some concessions where American vital interests were not directly affected. Moreover, he felt that when the sound and the fury had subsided, many problems could be resolved through calm discussion in a United Nations organization.

The divergent views of East and West were clearly revealed in the debate over the Polish issue, which was more controversial than any other at Yalta. Both the United States and Great Britain felt bound by the Atlantic Charter's pledge of self-determination. For their part, the Russians were influenced by considerations of national security. Twice within one generation, Stalin emphasized, Poland had been used as an invasion route to the Soviet Union, and the Poles themselves had attempted to seize the Ukraine in 1920. He was unwilling to risk an unfriendly government at his back door. Also, boundaries must be drawn in such a way as to offer protection for his country. In general, as Ambassador Averell Harriman had noted earlier, "The overriding consideration in Soviet foreign policy is the preoccupation with 'security.' The Soviet Union seeks a period of freedom from danger during which it can recover from the wounds of war and complete its industrial revolution." And in pursuing its objective it was not prepared to consider "the similar needs or rights of other countries."

The suggestion made by Roosevelt and Churchill that Poland's eastern boundary, known as the Curzon Line, be extended to permit Lwów and some of the oil fields to be included within Polish territory was categorically rejected by Stalin. That demarcation, he said, had been made in 1919 by Clemenceau and the Americans at Versailles, a conference to which the Russians had not been invited. Then he added passionately, "Now some people want that we should be less Russian than Curzon . . . and Clemenceau. . . . You would drive us into shame. . . . I could not take such a position and return to Moscow with an open face." It was finally agreed that the eastern boundary of Poland should follow the Curzon Line and the western boundary extend into German territory, the precise lines to be determined at the future peace conference.

The proposed composition of the Polish government provoked further controversy. There were currently two governments, the one in exile at London and the Soviet-sponsored one in Lublin, two armies, and two constitutions. To Roosevelt, the most practical course was to scrap both, establish a provisional body composed of representatives from London, from the Lublin group, and from among representative elements within Poland, and then schedule a free election as soon as possible. Churchill and Stalin both objected. The former contended that the London group should provide the leadership for the provisional government. The latter claimed that the London group was highly unpopular in Poland and out of touch with sentiment and conditions at home. Russia must have a neighbor, he said, which would be strong enough to "shut the door of this corridor [Poland] by her own force," as this was "not only a question of honor but of life and death for the Soviet state."

Both Roosevelt and Churchill remained firm in their opposition to the Lublin group, despite Molotov's claim that it enjoyed the enthusiastic support of the Polish people. The suggestion that it be enlarged to include some members of the exiled government proved equally unacceptable to the Russians. At last, Stalin agreed to Roosevelt's original recommendation that the provisional government remain in power only until free elections were held. When Roosevelt asked how soon this would be, Stalin replied within a month, barring the unlikely possibility of a catastrophe at the front. He refused to agree, however, to the President's proposal for international supervision of the elections. Instead, the British and American ambassadors would be permitted to investigate the situation to ascertain whether the pledge for bona fide elections had been fulfilled.

When the discussion was over, Roosevelt commented privately that he knew the agreement could be stretched by the Soviets to fit their purposes, but "it's the best I can do for Poland at this time." With the Red Army already in occupation of the country, the Western powers had little

choice. If Roosevelt had left Yalta without reaching an accord, what possibly could have prevented the Communist-led Lublin group from seizing control with Soviet assistance? And would the absence of any agreement have produced the desired free elections? At least a solemn promise was made, and responsibility for its breach could clearly be fixed.

Stalin also pledged free elections for the Balkan countries as soon as the occupying Nazis were ejected. In the Declaration on Liberated Europe, the Big Three agreed to "jointly assist the people in any European liberated state or former Axis satellite state" to establish peace and provide emergency relief, "to form interim governmental authorities broadly representative of all democratic elements in the population," and as soon as possible to establish through free elections "governments responsive to the will of the people." This statement promised a great deal but contained no machinery to establish such provisional governments or supervise early elections. The harsh fact was that implementation could be effected only by the power in military occupation, which, in this case, was the Soviet Union.

About Germany there was no prolonged argument. Stalin, desiring to neutralize the country permanently, asked that plans for dismemberment be formulated. Churchill stated that the issue was too complex to be settled in a few days, and Roosevelt's suggestion was accepted that the principle be endorsed but details worked out at a future conference of the foreign secretaries. Meanwhile, the northern part of East Prussia, including Königsberg, was to be turned over to the Soviets, the southern half to Poland, and the remainder of the country divided temporarily into four zones of occupation. Stalin had been strongly opposed to assigning a zone to the French, who "had opened the gates to the enemy," but finally yielded when Roosevelt informed him that the British would require help in the occupation as he did not believe the American people would consent to keep an army in Europe for more than two years. The city of Berlin, one hundred and ten miles within the Soviet zone, was also divided among the four occupying powers, with overall administration to be exercised by an inter-Allied governing authority.

The matter of reparations was thorny. All agreed that Germany should be expected to indemnify the Allies, but with about one-third of Soviet territory scorched and devastated and millions of Russians slaughtered, Stalin demanded huge reimbursements. He suggested a figure of twenty billion dollars to be obtained from foreign assets and industrial equipment. Churchill demurred that this would hopelessly impoverish the country, reducing the Germans to virtual starvation, and then "will we be required to keep them alive? If so, who is going to pay for that?" Roosevelt added that after the last war the United States poured billions of dollars into Germany, but "We cannot let that happen again." As with other issues, Roosevelt once again mediated, achieving a decision to turn the matter over to a reparations commission. During the conversations, the President's statement that the commission "should take [the sum of twenty billion dollars] in its initial studies as a basis for discussion," was later to be seized upon by the Russians as an indication that he had endorsed their position. But Roosevelt at no time committed himself to any specific figure.

For his consent to participate in the Pacific conflict, Stalin presented a number of demands designed to restore Russia as a major power in the Far East. He asked for and was granted the return of the territories and rights which Russia held before "the treacherous attack of Japan in 1904": the southern part of Sakhalin and adjacent islands, the lease of Port Arthur as a naval base, recognition of Russia's "preeminent interests" in the ice-free port of Dairen (which was to be internationalized), and re-establishment of joint operation with China of the Chinese-Eastern Railroad and the South Manchurian Railroad. In addition, the Kurile Islands were to be turned over to the Soviet Union, and the status quo in Outer Mongolia (the Mongolian People's Republic) was to be preserved.

In return for surrendering China's claims in Manchuria and Outer Mongolia, Roosevelt exacted a promise from Stalin that he would recognize Chinese sovereignty over Manchuria and support the Chinese Nationalist government in its struggle against Japan. In view of Russia's neutrality, the Far Eastern agreement was classified top secret and not made part of the Yalta protocol. Chiang Kai-shek was not consulted in advance, since it was feared that secrets could not be kept in Chungking, notorious for corruption and security leaks. It is doubtful whether the Generalissimo could have exacted better terms had he been present. Later, when the details of the agreement reached him, he approved them, welcoming a treaty of friendship and alliance with Russia which Stalin at Yalta told Roosevelt he would be willing to conclude. On August 14, 1945, a Sino-Soviet treaty was signed in Moscow containing the arrangements made with Stalin and officially establishing the postwar relations of the two nations.

Churchill, who did not participate in the Far Eastern negotiations, found the accord completely acceptable, declaring that he was "in favour of Russia's losses in the Russo-Japanese War being made good." Nevertheless, when the agreement was made public about a year later, it was more bitterly denounced than any other measure in Roosevelt's entire wartime diplomacy. Critics branded it as an appalling act of appeasement, claiming that the President had tossed away the gains achieved by military victory and that the balance of power in Asia had been altered in Russia's favor. In this instance, too, they ignored the limitations on Roosevelt's choices imposed by existing military realities.

A memorandum prepared by the War Department in April, 1945, analyzed the circumstances then prevailing. The concessions, it stated, "are within the military power of Russia to obtain regardless of U.S. military action short of war." The Soviet Union "was militarily capable of defeating the Japanese army deployed on the Chinese mainland and occupying Karafuto, Manchuria, Korea and Northern China" before American troops could reach those areas. Only in the Kuriles could the United States circumvent the Russians, but this would have to be "at the direct expense of the campaign to defeat Japan, and would involve an unacceptable cost in American lives." Furthermore, "the Russians can, if they choose, await the time when the United States' effort will have practically completed the destruction of Japanese military power and can then seize the objectives they desire at a cost to them relatively much less than would be occasioned by their entry into the war at an early date." In view of all this, the War Department concluded, "it appears we can bring little if any military leverage to bear on the Russians insofar as the Far East is concerned unless we choose to use force."

In consenting to the agreement, Roosevelt did not abandon the Chinese government but, on the contrary, was instrumental in having it accorded a position of high prestige in the international community. Through his efforts, China was included as one of the five permanent members in the United Nations Security Council when such recognition could be justified only by a sentimental regard for her fight against the Japanese, and not in terms of any ob-

jective standards of power. Though fully aware of the many limitations of Chiang Kai-shek's government, Roosevelt was determined to assist in its revitalization. In 1944, the President had sent General Patrick Hurley to China for conferences with Chiang and the Communists, hoping to achieve unity in the war against Japan. Hurley had succeeded in opening negotiations, but his efforts foundered on the refusal of both factions to agree on the nature and extent of government authority over the Communist troops. Moreover, he could not persuade Chiang to undertake a broadly based coalition government and a program of social and economic reform.

Fearing that civil war might again flare up after the defeat of Japan, with the Soviets assisting the Communists, Roosevelt desired to obtain Soviet endorsement and support for the Nationalist government. This he achieved at Yalta in the form of the promised pact of friendship and alliance, which he felt would also facilitate Chinese unification. If China's strength developed, it would act as a countervailing force checking Soviet ambitions in the Far East. Roosevelt never wavered in his loyalty to Nationalist China.

It is not likely that anything Roosevelt chose to do or not to do could have prevented the re-emergence of the Soviet Union as a Pacific power—Russia had formerly been one for more than a century and would naturally take advantage of the war situation to claim the territories taken from her by Japan. Roosevelt feared that an open break with the Soviet Union might destroy any possibility of bringing her into the United Nations and thus sacrifice the chance for a stable, peaceful world; nor would it thereby have prevented the extension of Soviet influence in the Far East.

The President operated within the framework of realistic alternatives as presented to him by his military advisers, including General Marshall, who was a brilliant strategist, and on the basis of advantages which he hoped would accrue to China through an agreement with the Soviets. Every statesman is frequently obliged to take a calculated risk. Roosevelt's actions were predicated on the assumption that China would become a viable state in the postwar period.

Each of the Big Three made and received concessions at the Crimea conference, but Roosevelt does appear to have been more conciliatory than the others. Exaggerating Allied dependence on the Soviets, he was apprehensive about jeopardizing the alliance. Though the situations in Eastern Europe and Asia were beyond his control, he could have attempted a more resolute stand, at least for the record. Perhaps Stalin, who mistook friendliness for weakness, might even have yielded to firmness on one point or another.

Two days before the conference ended, Stalin was host at a large dinner. The usual lengthy toasts exchanged by the three heads of state are highly revealing of their personalities and outlooks. The President declared that the dinner had a family atmosphere, which was how he liked to characterize relations among the three countries. Great changes had occurred in the world, he said, and greater changes were yet to come. It was their united purpose to give every human being the possibility of security and well-being. The Prime Minister toasted the President for his incalculable accomplishment in making possible an effective war against Hitler, though the United States had not been directly imperiled. Stalin struck a somber note. In toasting the alliance he declared that it was not difficult to maintain unity in wartime, while the desire to defeat the enemy provided a common bond; it was afterward that unity became strained by divergent and conflicting interests. He was confident, however, that this test would be

met and peacetime relations would continue on a friendly basis.

Churchill and Roosevelt left Yalta in a mood of high hope. Addressing the House of Commons, the realistic Prime Minister, who had always been hostile to the Soviet regime, was now sanguine about the future. "The impression I brought back from the Crimea, and from all my other contacts, is that Marshal Stalin and the Soviet leaders wish to live in honorable friendship and equality with the Western democracies. I feel also that their word is their bond. I know of no Government which stands to its obligations, even in its own despite, more solidly than the Russian Soviet Government," he declared.

The President was exultant that Yalta had laid down a solid foundation for winning the war and the peace. In his address to Congress on March 1, he asserted, "I may say we achieved a unity of thought and a way of getting along together. . . . Never before have the major Allies been more closely united—not only in their war aims but also in their peace aims." With his characteristic optimism and confidence in his ability to deal personally with any situation, Roosevelt was convinced that any future problems could be settled by sitting down around a conference table with Churchill and Stalin. Believing also that it would take years before the Soviet Union could recover from the appalling devastation the country had suffered, he had an exaggerated confidence in the Russians' eagerness to cooperate in the postwar period.

Yalta, then, was compounded of wartime exigencies and the fears and hopes that prevailed on the eve of victory. As the President saw it, the new world organization would provide both the atmosphere in which defects of wartime agreements could be remedied, and the framework within which American-Soviet cooperation could maintain the peace.

Suggestions for Further Reading

The literature on the Roosevelt diplomacy and World War II is vast, and there is no one-volume work of research and synthesis. The closest one can come to such a study is Robert A. Divine's Albert Shaw Lectures for 1968 at Johns Hopkins University, which have been published as *Roosevelt and World War II* (Baltimore, 1969) and focus on F.D.R.'s contribution to foreign policy. There are also the two surveys in the "America in Crisis" series published by John Wiley: Robert A. Divine, *The Reluctant Belligerent: American Entry into World War II* (New York, 1965), more than half of which covers the period from September 1939 to December 1941, and Gaddis Smith, *American Diplomacy During the Second World War, 1941–1945* (New York, 1965), which carries the story to the end of the war and briefly beyond. Though devoted only partly to the war years, two other studies worthy of mention are Willard Range, *Franklin D. Roosevelt's World Order* (Athens, Ga., 1959), which contends that F.D.R. worked consistently for particular ends in foreign affairs, especially during World War II, and Lloyd C. Gardner, *Economic Aspects of New Deal Diplomacy* (Madison, Wisc., 1964), which depicts Roosevelt's diplomacy as a continuation of traditional efforts to maintain an open-door policy throughout the world.

For the period from the outbreak of the war to Pearl Harbor, the student can begin with two essays that discuss writings on the causes of American involvement: Wayne S. Cole, "American Entry into World War II: A Historiographical Appraisal," *Mississippi Valley Historical Review*, XLIII (1957), 595–617, and Ernest R. May, *American Intervention: 1917 and 1941* (Washington, 1960). In addition to the extensive, scholarly accounts of William L. Langer and S. Everett Gleason, *The Challenge to Isolation,*

1937–1940 (New York, 1952) and *The Undeclared War, 1940–1941* (New York, 1953), there is a good, though less comprehensive survey of American diplomacy during this period in Donald F. Drummond, *The Passing of American Neutrality, 1937–1941* (Ann Arbor. Mich., 1955).

For two early pro-Administration explanations of war origins, see Forrest Davis and Ernest K. Lindley, *How War Came* (New York, 1942) and the volume published by the Department of State, *Peace and War: United States Foreign Policy, 1931–1941* (Washington, 1943). Charles Beard's *President Roosevelt and the Coming of the War, 1941* (New Haven, Conn., 1948), which gives the revisionist picture of the Roosevelt Administration as deliberately provoking American involvement against the wishes of the majority, should be preceded by his *American Foreign Policy in the Making, 1932–1940* (New Haven, Conn., 1946), in which he sets up the case made in the second book. Two other important early statements of the revisionist interpretation are: Charles C. Tansill, *Back Door to War: The Roosevelt Foreign Policy, 1933–1941* (Chicago, 1952,) and Harry Elmer Barnes (ed.), *Perpetual War for Perpetual Peace* (Caldwell, Idaho, 1953). Good examples of the partisan response to the revisionists are: Basil Rauch, *Roosevelt: From Munich to Pearl Harbor* (New York, 1950) and "History Through a Beard," in *By Land and By Sea: Essays and Addresses* by Samuel Eliot Morison (New York, 1953).

There is now a body of more specific and less passionate literature on the Roosevelt diplomacy, 1939–1941. On the domestic struggle to determine the response to the European war, there is Wayne S. Cole's study, *America First: The Battle Against Intervention, 1940–1941* (Madison, Wisc., 1953). *The Battle Against Isolation* (Chicago, 1944) by Walter Johnson is a good history of William Allen White's Committee to Defend America, though its tone is more in the spirit of the earlier defenses of the Roosevelt Administration mentioned above. Other more recent discussions of domestic attitudes toward foreign affairs can be found in Raymond H. Dawson, *The Decision to Aid Russia, 1941: Foreign Policy and Domestic Politics* (Chapel Hill, N.C., 1959); Robert Sobel, *The Origins of Interventionism: The United States and the Russo-Finnish War* (New York, 1960); Manfred Jonas, *Isolationism in America, 1935–1941* (Ithaca, N.Y., 1966); and Mark Chadwin, *Hawks of World War II* (Chapel Hill, N.C., 1968), a study of the most outspoken advocates of American intervention in 1940–1941. The revision of the neutrality law in 1939 is described in Robert Divine, *The Illusion of Neutrality* (Chicago, 1962). The Lend-Lease program is treated in Warren F. Kimball, *The Most Unsordid Act: Lend-Lease, 1939–1941* (Baltimore, 1969). The Atlantic Conference is discussed in Theodore A. Wilson, *The First Summit: Roosevelt and Churchill at Placentia Bay* (Boston, 1969). American relations with Germany are well covered in James V. Compton, *The Swastika and the Eagle: Hitler, the United States and the Origins of World War II* (Boston, 1967); Hans L. Trefousse, *Germany and American Neutrality, 1939–1941* (New York, 1951); Saul Friedländer, *Prelude to Downfall: Hitler and the United States, 1939–1941* (New York, 1967); and Alton Frye, *Nazi Germany and the American Hemisphere, 1931–1941* (New Haven, Conn., 1967).

Japanese-American relations before Pearl Harbor have now also been carefully studied. Though it limits itself to the years preceding those discussed in the present work, *The United States and the Far Eastern Crisis of 1933–1938* (Cambridge, Mass., 1964) by Dorothy Borg is highly useful in considering the questions raised in the Feis, Kubek and Schroeder contributions to this present work. Other valuable books on diplomatic developments are: F. C. Jones, *Japan's New Order in East Asia, 1937–1945* (London, 1954) and Robert J. C. Butow, *Tojo and the Coming of the War* (Princeton, N.J., 1961). Five useful articles emphasizing different aspects of how Japan and the United States got into war are: William L. Neumann, "How American Policy toward Japan Contributed to War in the

Pacific," in *Perpetual War for Perpetual Peace* edited by Harry Elmer Barnes (Caldwell, Idaho, 1953), pp. 231–268; Louis Morton, "The Japanese Decision for War," *United States Naval Institute Proceedings,* LXXX (1954), 1325–1335; Robert J. C. Butow, "The Hull-Nomura Conversations: A Fundamental Misconception," *American Historical Review,* LXV (1960), 822–836; and two in the *Mississippi Valley Historical Review:* Richard N. Current, "How Stimson Meant to 'Maneuver' the Japanese," XL (1953), 67–74, and Raymond A. Esthus "President Roosevelt's Commitment to Britain to Intervene in a Pacific War," L (1963), 28–38.

An introduction to the Pearl Harbor literature can be made through Louis Morton, "Pearl Harbor in Perspective: A Bibliographical Survey," *United States Naval Institute Proceedings,* LXXXI (1955), 461–468; Robert Ferrell, "Pearl Harbor and the Revisionists," *The Historian,* XVII (1955), 215–233; and Herbert Feis, "War Came at Pearl Harbor: Suspicions Considered," *Yale Review,* XLV (1956), 378–390. The case against the field commanders which gained currency during the war is made in Walter Millis, *This is Pearl!* (New York, 1947). The revisionist argument suggesting that Roosevelt foresaw and permitted the Pearl Harbor disaster as a means of unifying the country behind a direct part in the war is elaborated in Robert A. Theobald, *The Final Secret of Pearl Harbor* (New York, 1954) and Husband E. Kimmel, *Admiral Kimmel's Story* (Chicago, 1955). The results of the 1945–1946 congressional investigation of the Pearl Harbor attack are summarized in *Report of the Joint Committee on the Investigation of the Pearl Harbor Attack* (Washington, 1946). American intelligence operations and Pearl Harbor are analyzed in Roberta Wohlstetter, *Pearl Harbor: Warning and Decision,* (Stanford, Calif., 1962) and in Ladislas Farago, *The Broken Seal: The Story of "Operation Magic" and the Pearl Harbor Disaster* (New York, 1967).

Both the pre- and post-Pearl Harbor periods are rich in memoir and biographical literature about American foreign policy makers. *The Memoirs of Cordell Hull* (2 vols.; New York, 1948) can now be balanced by Julius Pratt, *Cordell Hull, 1933–1944,* vols. XII and XIII of *The American Secretaries of State and Their Diplomacy,* edited by Robert H. Ferrell and Samuel Bemis (New York, 1964), and Donald F. Drummond, "Cordell Hull, 1933–1944," in *An Uncertain Tradition: American Secretaries of State in the Twentieth Century,* edited by Norman A. Graebner (New York, 1961), 184–209. Robert E. Sherwood, *Roosevelt and Hopkins: An Intimate History* (New York, 1948) is a highly valuable source, particularly for the period of American belligerency. Roosevelt's Secretary of War Henry L. Stimson presents his views in Henry L. Stimson and McGeorge Bundy, *On Active Service in Peace and War* (New York, 1948). A sympathetic portrait of Stimson is given in Elting E. Morison, *Turmoil and Tradition: A Study of the Life and Times of Henry L. Stimson* (Boston, 1960), and a critical one in Richard N. Current, *Secretary Stimson: A Study in Statecraft* (New Brunswick, N.J., 1954). Secretary of the Treasury Henry Morgenthau, Jr.'s role in foreign policy forms part of the story in John M. Blum, *From the Morgenthau Diaries: Years of Urgency, 1938–1941* (Boston, 1965) and *Years of War, 1941–1945* (Boston, 1967).

Other memoirs and appraisals of important Roosevelt diplomats are: Under Secretary of State Sumner Welles, *The Time for Decision* (New York, 1944) and *Seven Decisions That Shaped History* (New York, 1951); Hull's successor, Secretary of State Edward R. Stettinius, Jr., *Roosevelt and the Russians: The Yalta Conference* (New York, 1949), and Walter Johnson, "Edward R. Stettinius, Jr., 1944–1945," in *An Uncertain Tradition,* pp. 210–222; James F. Byrnes, Roosevelt's head of the Office of Economic Stabilization and War Mobilization, tells about his experiences at Yalta in *Speaking Frankly* (New York, 1947) and about his whole public life in *All in One Lifetime* (New York, 1958); In *I Was There* (New York, 1950) Admiral William D. Leahy presents his memoirs as Roosevelt's ambassador to Vichy France and Personal Chief of Staff; Joseph C. Grew, ambassador to Japan, and Under and Acting Secretary of State during the last four months of Roosevelt's life, provides his recollections in *Ten Years in Japan, 1932–1942* (New York, 1944) and *Turbulent Era: A Diplomatic Record of Forty Years, 1904–1945* (2 vols.; Boston, 1952), while his whole career is now ably described in Waldo H. Heinrichs, Jr., *American Ambassador: Joseph C. Grew and the Devel-*

opment of the United States Diplomatic Tradition (Boston, 1966); Robert Murphy discusses his important wartime diplomatic assignments dealing with Vichy, Italian surrender, and German occupation in *Diplomat Among Warriors* (New York, 1964); wartime relations with Russia are recorded in William H. Standley and Arthur A. Ageton, *Admiral Ambassador to Russia,* (Chicago, 1955), John R. Deane, *The Strange Alliance: The Story of Our Efforts at Wartime Cooperation with Russia* (New York, 1947) and George F. Kennan, *Memoirs, 1925–1950* (Boston, 1967).

For American diplomacy from Pearl Harbor to Roosevelt's death in April 1945, the reader does well to begin with Herbert Feis's comprehensive studies: *Churchill, Roosevelt, Stalin: The War They Waged and the Peace They Sought* (Princeton, N.J., 1957) and *The China Tangle: The American Effort in China from Pearl Harbor to the Marshall Mission* (Princeton, N.J., 1953).

A few examples of the revisionist critique of Roosevelt's wartime diplomacy in general and the Yalta agreements in particular are: Eugene Lyons, "Appeasement in Yalta," *American Mercury* (1945), 461–68; John T. Flynn, *While You Slept: Our Tragedy in Asia and Who Made It* (New York, 1951); and G. N. Crocker, *Roosevelt's Road to Russia* (Chicago, 1959). The revisionists are answered both directly and indirectly in a number of the works cited in this bibliography, but a good beginning can be made with John L. Snell (ed.), *The Meaning of Yalta* (Baton Rouge, La., 1956).

As with the pre-Pearl Harbor period, there are now a number of valuable special studies for the war years. A provocative interpretation of American war aims is offered in Gabriel Kolko, *The Politics of War: The World and United States Foreign Policy, 1943–1945* (New York, 1968). Among those evaluating the unconditional surrender policy are: Anne Armstrong, *Unconditional Surrender: The Impact of the Casablanca Policy upon World War II* (New Brunswick, N.J., 1961); Herbert Feis, *Churchill, Roosevelt, Stalin: The War They Waged and the Peace They Sought* (Princeton, N.J., 1957); and Paul Kecskemeti, *Strategic Surrender: The Politics of Victory and Defeat* (Stanford, Calif., 1958). American wartime policy toward Germany is treated in John L.

Snell, *Wartime Origins of the East-West Dilemma Over Germany* (New Orleans, 1959). William L. Langer, *Our Vichy Gamble* (New York, 1947) deals sympathetically with American policy toward defeated France, 1940–1942. American efforts to build a postwar peace-keeping body are described in Ruth B. Russell, *A History of the United Nations Charter: The Role of the United States, 1940–1945* (Washington, 1958) and in Robert A. Divine, *Second Chance: The Triumph of Internationalism in America During World War II* (New York, 1967). *America's Failure in China, 1941–1950* (Chicago, 1963) is analyzed by Tang Tsou. Relations with Latin America are discussed in Donald M. Dozer, *Are We Good Neighbors? Three Decades of Inter-American Relations, 1930–1960* (Gainesville, Fla., 1959).

American wartime diplomacy cannot be fully understood without a study of military planning. The literature here is vast, but there are a handful of useful general discussions: Hanson W. Baldwin, *Great Mistakes of the War* (New York, 1950); Samuel E. Morison, *Strategy and Compromise* (Boston, 1958); Kent R. Greenfield (ed.), *Command Decisions* (Washington, 1960); and Greenfield, *American Strategy in World War II: A Reconsideration* (Baltimore, 1963); also an essay on Franklin Roosevelt by William Emerson in *The Ultimate Decision: The President as Commander in Chief*, edited by Ernest R. May (New York, 1960). For more detailed information, there is the "United States Army in World War II" series published by the U.S. Government Printing Office. The most useful volumes in this series for the reader of this problem book are in the subseries entitled "The War Department" and "The Western Hemisphere." Samuel E. Morison's multivolume *History of United States Naval Operations in World War II* is summarized in *The Two-Ocean War* (Boston, 1963).

The published documentary record of American diplomacy during the war is now considerable. The best introductions to this material are through Louis Morton, "Sources for the History of World War II," *World Politics*, XIII (1961), 435–453, and the more general article by Richard W. Leopold, "The Foreign Rela-

tions Series: A Centennial Estimate," *Mississippi Valley Historical Review*, XLIX (1963), 595–612, especially, 603–609. Deserving of special mention are: the Department of State history, *Postwar Foreign Policy Preparation, 1939–1945* (Washington, 1949); *Foreign Relations of the United States: The Conferences at Cairo and Teheran, 1943* (Washington, 1961); and *The Conferences at Malta and Yalta, 1945* (Washington, 1955); also, *Correspondence between the Chairman of the Council of Ministers of the U.S.S.R. and the Presidents of the U.S.A. and the Prime Ministers of Great Britain during the Great Patriotic War of 1941–1945* (2 vols., Moscow, 1957), and a commentary on this publication by Herbert Feis, "The Three Who Led," *Foreign Affairs*, XXXVII (1959), 282–292.

Finally, there are a number of important works which treat the Roosevelt diplomacy in a larger context. A useful survey is John L. Snell, *Illusion and Necessity: The Diplomacy of Global War, 1939–1945* (Boston, 1963). The most important British works are Winston Churchill's history, *The Second World War* (6 vols.; Boston, 1948–1953); *The Memoirs of Anthony Eden: The Reckoning* (Boston, 1965); Arthur Bryant, *The Turn of the Tide* and *Triumph in the West* (London, 1957 and 1959), based on the diaries of General Sir Alan Brooke, Chief of the Imperial General Staff; William H. McNeill, *America, Britain and Russia: Their Co-operation and Conflict, 1941–1946* (London, 1953), which is one of the eleven volumes in the valuable *Survey of International Affairs, 1939–1946* (London, 1952–1958); Sir Llewellyn Woodward, *British Foreign Policy in the Second World War* (London, 1962), an official history drawn from British Foreign Office records; and J. R. M. Butler (ed.), *Grand Strategy* (6 vols.; London, 1955–1964), which is part of the United Kingdom military series in the official British history of World War II. For relations with France and Italy from a non or not strictly American perspective, see Charles de Gaulle, *War Memoirs* (3 vols.; New York, 1955–1960); Arthur Funk, *Charles de Gaulle: The Crucial Years, 1943–1944* (Norman, Okla.; 1959); and Norman Kogan, *Italy and the Allies* (Cambridge, Mass., 1956).